THE CREATIVE AMBUSH

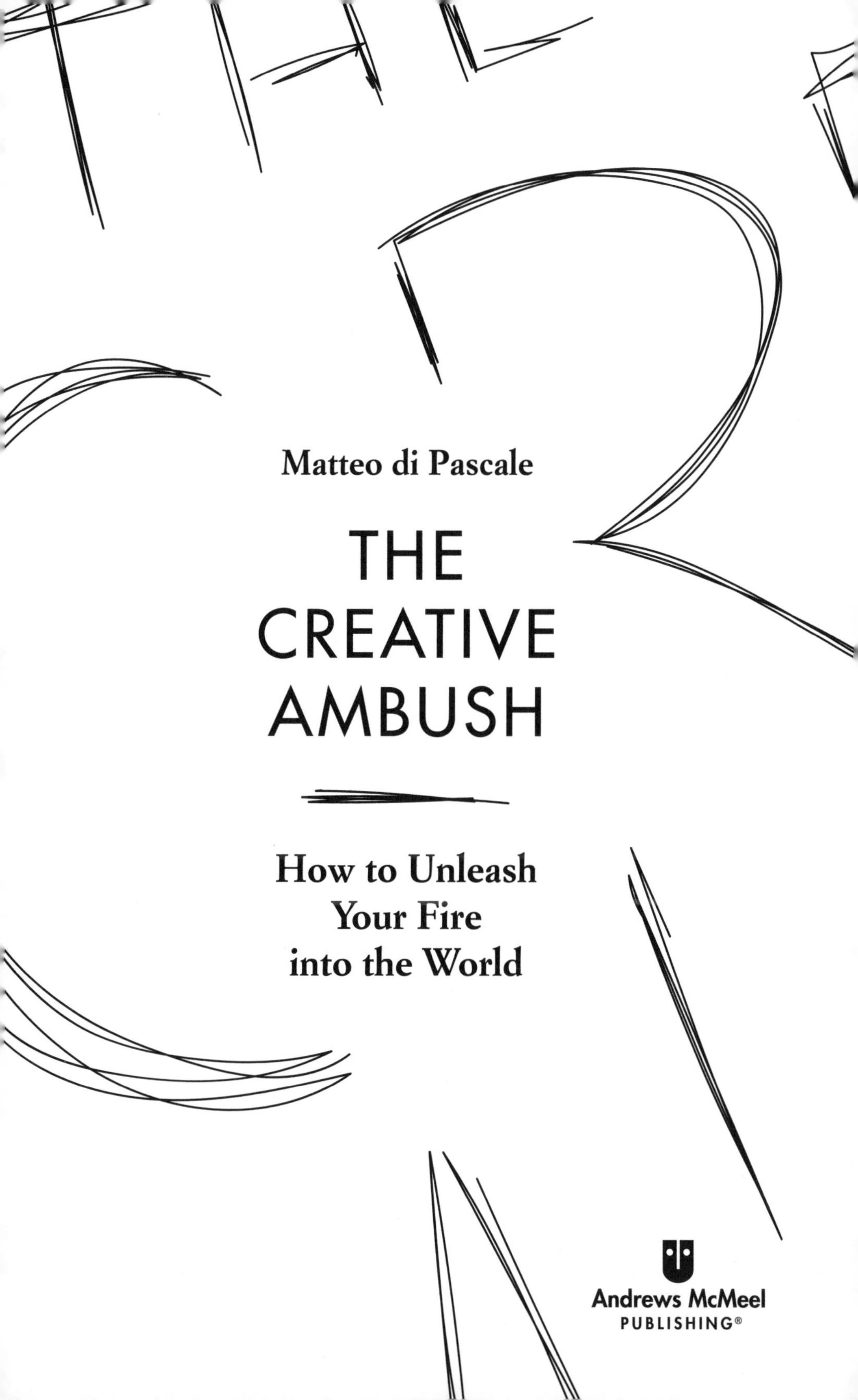

Matteo di Pascale

THE CREATIVE AMBUSH

How to Unleash Your Fire into the World

Andrews McMeel
PUBLISHING®

The authorised representative in the EEA is Simon and Schuster Netherlands BV, Herculesplein 96 3584 AA Utrecht, Netherlands. (info@simonandschuster.nl)

Andrews McMeel Publishing
a division of Andrews McMeel Universal
1130 Walnut Street, Kansas City, Missouri 64106

www.andrewsmcmeel.com

Originally published in Italian, *Agguato creativo* by Sefirot Independent Publishers in 2024. Translation by Alizé Latini.

Cover photo by Davide Menarello. Cover art by Matteo di Pascale.

25 26 27 28 29 SDB 10 9 8 7 6 5 4 3 2 1

Hardback ISBN: 979-8-8816-0422-6
Paperback ISBN: 979-8-8816-0421-9

Library of Congress Control Number: 2025933725

Editor: Jean Z. Lucas
Art Director/Designer: Julie Barnes
Production Editor: Dave Shaw
Production Manager: Chuck Harper

Contents

DISCLAIMER

What is this book and who is it for?

This is not simply a handbook on creativity. It is something more: It is a laugh-out-loud, earthshaking book, a shake-up that will challenge you and force you to experience the thrill of creative life, its ups and downs, the pain of falling on your ass, and the extraordinary excitement of feeling your hands burning hot, driven by the eagerness to create something new. Those who will have the courage and the strength to get up time and time again, to laugh and enjoy the trembling of their knees as the vibration rises to the sky, those are the readers to whom this book is dedicated.

The Creative Ambush is for all of those who want to feel creative and wish to pursue the creative path whether you are a professional, an artist (art director, designer, illustrator, painter, writer, sculptor, etc.), or simply a creative soul (manager, entrepreneur, chef, teacher, employee, shoemaker, baker . . . and I could go on and on and on with this list). The important thing is that you wish to access the dimension where creating, breaking patterns, finding new solutions, intuition, and miracles exist.

If you are among those who often say, "No, I'm absolutely not creative!," you can put the book down. Don't read it; it is not for you, yet. Maybe you bought it by mistake or it was a gift, in which case give it to someone who you know can benefit from it.

But if you feel a burning desire, a fire that you want to feed and free upon the world, you must keep going: This *is* the book for you.

Introduction

I usually start my lectures by asking, "What is creativity?"

And I get a wide array of answers: Creativity is talent, it is the ability to come up with ideas; creativity is expressing yourself, it is creating something that did not exist before; it is passion, love for what you do, becoming a channel for something higher . . .

That's when I insist: Is a designer who invents a new tool more creative than an advertiser who spits out fifty ideas an hour? Is the artist who paints a wonderful painting more creative than the actress who brings a character to life? Is the young startup founder who studies a food delivery app more creative than the person who invents a new pasta dish?

Was Picasso more creative than the person who invented pizza? Da Vinci or Bill Gates? Castaneda or Ogilvy? The creator of a new teaching method or the one who invented the ballpoint pen?

As some of you have already guessed, these are funny questions to get the ball rolling, nothing more than tricks. After letting the answers roll for a while, I explain that *creativity* is such a versatile, flexible, and overused term that there is no right or wrong definition.

However, since it is *my* lecture (ha ha)—in this case it is my book—we'll embrace my vision of creativity, which is the most extensive possible: Creativity is to create something new.

First it wasn't there and now it is. Poof. Like magic. And it can be of any shape and size. In fact, for me there is no difference between a writer and a chef, between an artist and a middle school teacher: If they express themselves, they are creative.

I'm super proud of my bread recipe (buckwheat and chick-pea flour, no yeast) just as I'm proud of my stories. I worked hard to find the right combination of ingredients; I studied and then tested it out dozens of times, and every time I see the bread rise, or when someone sees a picture and asks for the recipe, I feel extremely proud of my creation.

I am a creative. I have dedicated my life to self expression, to the task of bringing out something that was inside of me. I've always felt a push toward creating, building, developing, and generating new things.

I have done many things: I worked as an art director and UX designer for companies and agencies in Milan, Turin, Amsterdam, and Shenzhen, for brands like Samsung, OnePlus, and Whirlpool; I built the first UX design online academy in Italy; I published a few novels; I wrote *Survival Guide for UX Designers*, the highest-selling book of its kind in Italy; I developed the creative tools intùiti, Fabula Deck, Fabula Deck for Kids, Cicero, Edito, BAD; and when I couldn't convince a single publishing house to include them in their catalogs, I founded Sefirot, my own publishing house, through which I sold more than one hundred fifty thousand units all over the world.

I've had a brilliant career, and the truth is I've never been the best UX designer or the greatest art director or the best writer, either of fiction or nonfiction. There are so many people out there who are more dedicated than me, more specialized, more talented. Yet I always had a burning longing—the yearning to express myself and never having enough of it, of wanting to break the cage I felt closing too tight around me—and I think this was the key to my success and satisfaction.

At work they liked me because they sensed I had a strength that couldn't be contained and that I impatiently had to use it. The UX manual had a following because it is a quirky, straightforward, fun product, full of illustrations that bring smiles to the reader's face. Sefirot shines because it is different and had the courage to publish titles that no one believed in.

There is no formula for this, no mathematical equation or framework to lean on. I had the courage and arrogance to expand into the world, and something good happened. And my intention, with the help of this book, is to push you to do the same, to challenge yourself, to find out what you really have to give, in any field, and also to face disappointment if the result should be less glorious than you expected.

A master can only take those who follow as far as they have come, no further than that, and it has taken me almost two decades to become my favorite creative.

I want to take you there: I want you to become your favorite creative.

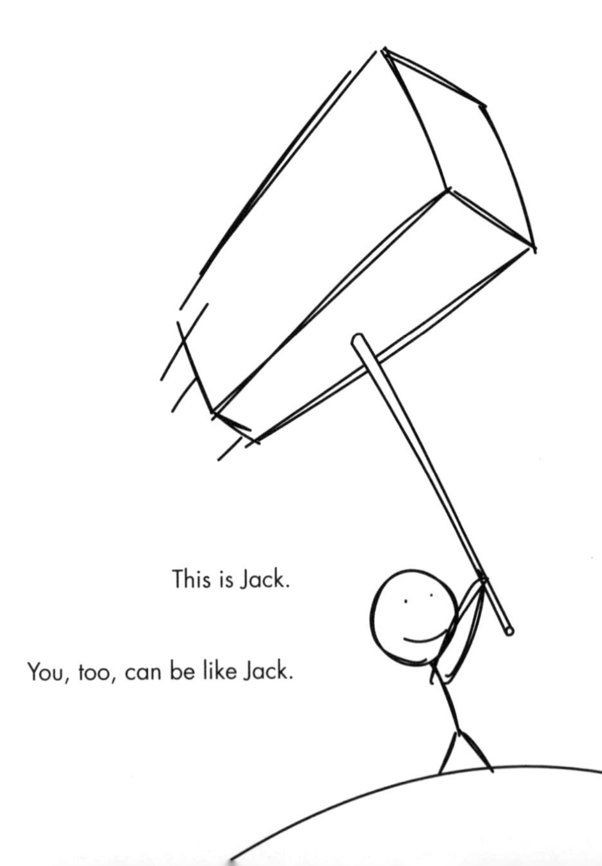

This is Jack.

You, too, can be like Jack.

PART I

To Demolish

Rebellion

Years ago I went to a job interview for an advertising company in Turin (maybe the most famous), and I met with the head of HR and her assistant. They smiled at me while we sat around a shiny crystal table set in a basement meeting room that looked like the VIP area of a club. They wanted me—they made it clear from the start—because I had already worked in Leo Burnett, another famous agency. For them, that was reassuring enough since ad agencies are cutthroat meat grinders, and they wanted someone who they thought could survive the metal teeth of that hellish machine.

But their smiles slowly disappeared when I told them that I had quit Leo Burnett. They looked at my résumé, reading it with more attention than before, and there it was, ink on paper: It said that it had been months since I had worked there.

The manager picked up her glasses. "Why," she asked, "did you leave?" When I told her that I didn't like the quality of the output, the final result of the work I spent so much time on, she looked over at her colleague aghast, as if she was talking with a madman. I laughed out loud.

"And would you like to go back and work in an ad agency?" she asked. I leaned forward. "It depends on what you offer and most of all on what I will be doing," I answered.

The lights dimmed for a moment, as if I had dared to curse in that seventy-year-old Temple of Advertising. The head of HR took a breath and looked like she was about to faint, and for a moment, I honestly thought the assistant was going to grab her in her arms. It seemed like she was mumbling the words: "What? Isn't working for such an important firm not enough for you? I mean, it is for *us*!"

"If I end up making shit"—I didn't say that, I used *things I don't like* instead of *shit*—"the answer is no, it is not enough." I imagined the dialogue between them: "Oh my god, Maria, this is the kind of guy who quits unexpectedly, without a logical reason."

The manager straightened her back in the chair, her lips slowly paralyzed in a grimace that locked the side of her mouth; she took pen and paper and drew two circles. She handed it to me, like I was a child and said, "So, if some special projects, which I can't talk about, get the green light—she hit the first circle—you would work with the creative team on those, otherwise—she hit the second circle—you would work with our regular clients."

I looked at her, feeling confused. That didn't explain the position at all. She let her fingers run through her hair. "Oh," she complained, "I don't understand why you creative people always have to make it hard. Why do you care so much about what you do? Don't we pay you to do it? Then do it."

It was at that exact moment, while the head of HR lectured me and her assistant nodded proudly, that I decided I was going to turn this interview upside down.

"Let me teach you something," I said.

I took a piece of paper from the stack sitting at the center of the table. I folded it in two. I tore it and slipped one half toward the senior and the other toward the junior.

"By noon you have to fill this with something, and I'll come back to evaluate it." They stared at those white rectangles looking terrified. "Perfect," I said, "you will then go to lunch, and at two o'clock I will hand you a sheet that must be filled in by the evening, and I will evaluate what you wrote. And tomorrow we will do the same, and the day after that, and the day after that, and so on."

"Feeling anxious? I know . . ." I said. "And it mustn't be some mechanical thing, a repetitive action. You must pour your entire self into every blank piece of paper. Every day."

They looked at me flabbergasted, like I was a monster.

"And you dare to ask us why we creatives want to do something we like? Because deciding to employ ourselves totally into useless things kills us."

I looked at the pieces of paper I handed them, and I realized that, yes, just like a piece of paper you might end up being consumed and scattered in the wind.

They didn't call me back of course.

Magic and responsibility

Potentially, we are all magicians who hold the power of the infinite, yet unrealized, possibilities in our hands. This is creativity. We can feel something new, and then we see it, we think about it, we create it. We can build it, write it, play it, sing it. We have this incredible power that we should never underestimate. We can create something new, isn't that wonderful?

It is pure magic: An idea that descends from above, coming from who knows where, awakens us or catches us by surprise while we walk on the street. I am talking about inspiration and intuition, and the urge to chase them when they suggest something to us. It is a spectacular and mysterious dimension, powerful and inexplicable, that needs acceptance more than explanation, a desire to plunge in, get involved, and experience it.

Be careful, though: As I was telling the two HR employees in the agency, it is a power that comes with a certain degree of intensity, through which we pour ourselves into what we do, so we must have care and respect for it, otherwise we end up creating blocks upon blocks that hold back the mechanism until it stops in its tracks, leaving us feeling like plastic bottles squeezed until we are empty.

We will start this journey from the blocks. We all have them: Usually, they are made up of sentences and concepts that limit us, both coming from the outside and from those teachings that we have internalized and that we repeat to ourselves like mantras.

If you have a project, whether it is writing a book, creating a board game, opening a café, changing jobs, making music, or any other thing that makes you happy and vibrant, and you're not doing it, or at least not pursuing it the way you would like—for example you are already writing a book or working as an art director, but you can't put your entire self into it—there's nothing to worry about: It happens to us all.

The thing is, there is a block somewhere and all we have to do is take it apart.

This is the most unpleasant part because if we are pushing on the brakes, there must be a reason. If we are climbing up with a rope so tight that it's cutting into our waist preventing us from reaching the top, it is because we are afraid of falling. Removing some of our blocks will be painful and annoying; it will make us shiver, it will make us cry; however, we must remember that if we keep those limits, we will never be able to fly. But I guarantee that once we remove them, the joy of freedom will seize us like a wind filled with creative fury, and our internal voice will tell us, "You can do whatever you want, so do it!"

External blocks

Let's start with the external blocks. We are going to shake things up a bit. There is a huge need to destroy, to throw away old systems, catchphrases, preconstructed ideas, until we realize that there are no more patterns, that everything is possible.

That is, after all, the starting point of creativity.

If we were to rebel against a religion, we would try to be as blasphemous as possible; we would dare to demolish the dogmas, the commandments of creativity, those concepts that are taken for granted and are now repeated over and over again, used on social media, by professors in universities, by great designers and employers alike.

So get a hammer, muster some courage, and follow me: We are going to shoot at the sky, plant bombs, and build a new world. It will be a lot of fun.

1) Not everyone wants to be creative

Let's say it out loud: Creativity is a trend. It is treated as a soft skill, a cross-cutting skill that gives an edge to those who claim to "have it." One of the most overused positive catchphrases is: "We are all creative," which is often said with a sense of self-righteousness, as if creativity is an inalienable right and a hand should be extended to the more shy to reassure them, to tell them that, "Yes, you can be creative too."

Creative inclusion, which is often enforced through workshops and meetings, involves the use of techniques such as colored voting stickers, sticky notes, moments for thinking, and moments dedicated to sharing to make sure that everyone, even the most hesitant, gets a chance to have their say and make a contribution. A true automatization of the creative process to make it accessible to all.

The underlying democratic ideal is to restrain the most charismatic individuals from hogging the conversation so that those who are by nature less imposing are included as well; the capitalist ideal, on the other hand, which is what drives companies to pay for this kind of workshop, is to maximize team contributions, forcing all the chickens to hatch, even the most reluctant ones.

Now let's make an effort to look around the meeting table, and we will see the ugly truth: Not everyone wants to be creative.

Albert over there is thinking that it is getting late and in twenty minutes he wants to get out of there so he can pick up his daughter from school, and Susan next to him, who decided to pursue a career as an account manager precisely because she has always considered herself more rational than creative, just wants to do her thing and then go to the gym; neither of them really feels like being creative right now. They have their own reasons to have no desire to fill a blank sheet of paper with thoughts and ideas. And yes, sure, they, too, might contribute in some way to the brainstorming that is taking place at the table, they might be useful if forced to hatch, but they don't care about what's being done. Maybe they want to be creative in another way and in another place (maybe he wants to compose music at home after dinner), or maybe they have decided not to venture down the unpredictable road of creativity (maybe she suffers from anxiety and prefers to operate in more definite, clear-cut, tangible territories), and it is only fair that they can be free to quietly sit at the brainstorming table minding their own business while those who want to be creative monopolize the conversation.

But let's turn our attention to John, who is sitting on the opposite side of the table, listening to Lucy and Valerie with pure admiration; those two look like they could physically fight each other to defend their ideas. You can tell that John would like to raise his hand to announce that, yes, he, too, has had an intuition and has a proposal to make, but his arm wavers, he doesn't dare: Is he lacking the energy or the courage?

So what should we do? Stop everything, ask everyone to be quiet, hand out ten sets of sticky notes, force those at the table to jot down their ideas, and then finally give John the space he democratically deserves?

John is not the victim here. John is a grown man who is acting like a child. Yes, there is such a thing as creative responsibility: Raise your hand, open your mouth, have the courage to say the stupidest thing ever while everyone looks at you, and then, if you didn't talk only for the pleasure of hearing the sound of your own voice, find a second dose of courage and defend your idea. It is far from simple: You sweat, your face turns red, your heart skips a couple of beats. It takes tremendous courage to be creative, and you have to want it badly. When you are a child, it is okay for a teacher to help you out, to push you a bit; when you are an adult, it is not.

There are people like Susan who simply do not want to be creative, others who want to be creative at a certain moment, like Albert, and people who would like to be creative but decide not to, like John. There is no right or wrong. Not everyone has to come up with ideas, write books, compose songs, paint, innovate, create. It is not mandatory. Not only that: Those who decide to be creative are no better than those who don't want to be.

And besides, it is not our problem. Everyone has their reasons for choosing to be a certain way, and it is only fair that they take responsibility for it.

We shouldn't feel bad for those who seem to want to but can't, like John. If he can't find the strength to do it, to commit himself, to get out of his box, that's his damn business. We're not in his head, we don't know what he really thinks while sitting on his chair with his fist clenched: Maybe he is convinced that he has to say something in order to not be left out; maybe he is so arrogant that he believes he doesn't even have to share his pearls of wisdom with Lucy and Valerie.

Breakdown no. 1

Let's drop the cheap do-goodism, leave others to their own devices, and focus on the only variable we can work on: ourselves.

Think about your responsibility.

The only certain thing is this: If we do not express ourselves, whatever the reason, deep down we do not want to be creative, and we cannot be saved. No one will ever come and lend us a hand.

We have to tend it to ourselves. There is no pouting and sulking; creativity is not a right we can get by stamping our feet. It is up to us to decide.

We have to be the ones who want to be creative.

2) Framework, lateral thinking, and other tricks will not make us creative

There is a lot of talk about ways to increase or develop creativity: methods, strategies, frameworks, structures. I myself have enormous fascination and respect for these kinds of solutions, and I have developed several tools with Sefirot, my publishing company, in the form of cards that you can arrange on the wall and use with sticky notes, such as Fabula Deck for writers or BAD Canvas for designers and entrepreneurs.

Any help is valid and welcome. The problem lies in the misunderstanding that the tools will turn people into creatives. They merely provide help to better channel a certain drive.

During presentations of Fabula Deck, a tool that offers a framework for writing novels and screenplays based on the hero's journey, there is always someone who raises their hand and asks the fateful question: "Okay, this sounds great, but who is going to actually write the story?"

Well, love, you're the one who has to write it.

All those frameworks and methods are merely complex knowledge synthesized and offered to simplify actions. Fabula Deck will not turn you into a writer overnight, just as Design Thinking does not turn you into a master designer, and the same goes for Design Sprint, Business Model Canvas, Lean Canvas, and so on. They are simplified ways to get from point A to point B, which allow us to find the faster road, maybe make fewer turns; however, they do not give us the car, the gasoline, nor the will to travel.

Those are things we must put in ourselves.

It is the same misunderstanding with lateral thinking codified by Edward de Bono. Solving problems by tackling them from the side, laterally, instead of head-on, by finding alternatives, by searching into the world of the absurd, switching vision and perspectives. These are all valid, applicable, and effective suggestions, but it is the promise with which they are perceived that tricks us: to be creative with as little effort as possible. That illusory joy of having found the grail, the pot of gold, the system for turning on creativity with a snap of the fingers, with a magic technique, with a new way to conduct a brainstorming session.

Have you ever done a real brainstorming session? Knowing about the existence of brainstorming never made anyone more creative. Ha ha. It doesn't work that way. Getting into brainstorming means to walk into discomfort—it is the knowledge that we are testing ourselves over and over again until we have found a good idea. Of course we can use "divergent thinking" first to come up with a large number of ideas, then we will use "convergent thinking" to narrow down what we have and keep the best ideas. Okay, but do we really think that coding the uncodifiable can give us power over it? Truth is, after three hours of brainstorming, on the fourth straight day, when we realize that none of the ideas are even acceptable, we will take all of the words that our comfort zone loves so much, and we will shove it up where the sun doesn't shine. What can we *converge* on, when only shit has come out of *diverging*?

We will find ourselves walking around, taking cold showers, talking about it over and over as we come to terms with the one and only truth: We will never have control over creativity, no matter how many techniques, neologisms, and magic spells we can come up with. We will also understand why we feel the strong urge to find systems to latch on to: because it is terrifying knowing that we have no control, that we must abandon ourselves to the kind of flow one can learn to navigate but will never tame.

No creative person, no matter how senior they are, knows that something good will always come out of a meeting. No writer knows that the book will actually become reality. The experience doesn't guarantee the chance to bend ideas, but it does teach how to respect this immense and unknown force.

It is not the water that learns how to bend to the will of the sailor. It is the sailor who has learned to respect the water.

Breakdown no. 2

Let's make a list of the tools we use—books, canvas, methods, AI—to be creative.

Would we be able to work without them? Do we simply depend on these tools, or are we slaves to them?

Let's imagine the tools set on the table in front of us or in the room. Feel how different they are from us; they are not part of us, they are part of an external reality.

Thank them for what they've given you and imagine pushing them away, making them small or even kicking them out of the room. We can use gestures, make a sound, or take a deeper breath if that helps.

Feel that you are the creative one, you are your only tool. We'll never be confused again: We are the only ones capable of doing so. At that point, we can use any instrument, framework, game, method to help us, but it will never again define our creativity.

It is ours and ours only.

You are tools, and I thank you.
I take my power back, and I will never again delegate my creativity to something outside of me.

3) Creativity is not a mechanical method (nor a muscle that needs training)

Another trend right now is teaching creativity as if it were something accessible, structurable (or even worse, already structured), or codifiable, that can be put into a system and then shared. I can teach you the equation for ideas, and you can put it into practice at home. Two plus two equals creativity. That's clearly bullshit: another rope to hang on to to feel less lost in an unpredictable world. Making the concept as simple as possible: Creativity is to create something new, be it a product, a new system to achieve a result, a solution to a problem, or a breaking of old paradigms. To make something that wasn't there before and now it is.

But where do ideas come from? How does something shape inside of us, an image or a sentence, a vision (for the few fortunate ones) that we suddenly need to chase? Whether it is an electrical discharge between neurons or the voice of God or a demon whispering in our ear, the only certainty is that we cannot force this process. We cannot sit in a chair and order our brain or a higher entity, "Chop-chop, give me a good idea." Try it out and see if it works. Enlightenment comes when we least expect it, while we are in the shower, or on the way home from work, or out of nowhere without even having started nor mentioned brainstorming. First there was emptiness and then poof there was enlightenment.

I wracked my brain for weeks to find the name for a storytelling tool. I talked about it with my business partner on the phone. We would say names out loud, just to hear what they sounded like, even though, as we said them, we already knew they weren't the right ones. Names like *Storytellers* but maybe without the *e* to make it smarter, *Storytellrs*. I kept on shouting names alone in the car, or walking back and forth from the office: dozens, hundreds, thousands of names, one more appalling and inadequate than the other.

And then one evening, while having dinner at a friend's house, we opened Google looking for synonyms for the word *plot,* and the third choice on the site was *fabula.* When I saw those six letters, I felt two separate things connecting somewhere, a beam of light coming down and putting everything back together. I said it out loud, "Fabula!" The others looked at me, and I repeated it, knowing that it was the right name and that my partner would agree, "Fabula! Fuck, Fabula is perfect, it's beautiful."

I have known the difference between fabula and plot since high school, yet that word had not occurred to me during all the brainstorming sessions. Could it be that the system was working in the warm darkness of my unconscious mind, and that at some point the final idea came out of the wall of black smoke? Or maybe there was an alignment in the universe, and a star came down and hit me on the head? If I had taken a cold shower or slept eight hours a night, would it have hit me sooner?

Do we really need to know? I don't think so. How about we stay on the magical feeling that strikes us when a new idea arrives? It's pure joy, as if a thread had finally been pulled somewhere and we feel connected to everything, the pieces fall into place, the glory that excites us is not so much related to ego; it's more of an emotional outburst, a child laughing and crying at the same time. Those who have experienced it know that it is a wonderful feeling. It nourishes us and makes us feel what fullness is.

Now you see how ideas cannot be forced to appear. At most, we can wish for them to arrive. And the worst part of creativity is the space between an idea and another, when we stand in between flames, when we walk miserably in front of a temple, and we don't know how long it will take before they will let us in. Try using lateral thinking or thinking hats now, or any other tool. It won't do you any good except to give you the illusion that you are doing something, that you still have a say in the matter.

And this wandering around with the hidden fear of doing nothing but fumbling in the dark will always be there. It is happening to me right now, as I write this book and I don't really know where I'm going with it; I can only dive in and trust that something will keep happening, that at the end of each chapter I'll be hooked on the next one, and that the whole bundle will reveal itself at some point.

Breakdown no. 3

Let's break the link that ties us with the mechanical view of creativity. Let's see the absurdity (and also the lack of poetry and heart) inherent in that American-style way of doing things that expects willpower to be everything, that everything depends solely and exclusively on our commitment and discipline.

That's not how it goes: Not everything depends on willpower. You've been fed another illusion: Creativity is way bigger and more unmanageable.

Let's try to change our attitude: What if our commitment was not to squeeze, force, and destroy ourselves, but to open ourselves to something higher, to be willing to believe, to receive, to rely on a dimension—where inspiration and ideas live—that we cannot know and control?

What if the purpose wasn't so much about doing but reaching something?

Imagine walking in front of a temple, our inner temple standing in an open space. It's night and the sky is starry. We feel that the creative process is not an endless working factory but an intimate place where we can dare to ask, "Wow, that is different, right?"

So let's do it for real, let's try, let's ask for something: an idea, an inspiration. Let's try to have the experience of relying on something higher.

4) Chosen ones exist . . . but why should we care?

"You either have it or you don't," "You can't learn to write, either you're a writer or you aren't," "Either you have talent and you were born with it, or you can't do anything about it."

Are you familiar with this kind of mindset?

We read similar sentences constantly under Fabula's social media posts: Hundreds of people can't wait to write things like, "You don't need anything in order to be a writer," "If you don't know how to write, go peel potatoes," "Even the courses are useless," and a bunch of similar bullshit.

These sentences are very limiting and point toward a nihilism in which nothing makes sense unless you are born under the right star, a world where genius and talent are innate gifts granted from above, and therefore, there are the chosen ones, the people destined for greatness, and the outcasts who, despite their efforts, just have to suck it up and stand aside.

It is an exhausting and discouraging current of thought, the same one that prompts a parent to say to their child, "Do you really want to be a writer? An artist? A singer? Only one in a million succeeds." As if to say: You're either chosen by the stars or you're shit. This approach has the power to make us feel useless and to tempt us into giving up and say, "Okay, I don't have that gift, so there's no point in putting any effort in it."

I fell for it big time: In my twenties, I was obsessed with this thought, and I repeated over and over a passage that said, "Goethe had a demon in his ear that advised him," and . . . I wanted it too! The first question I asked of the tarot cards when I met my spiritual teacher was: "Am I blessed with literary genius?" I didn't even know what this genius was, but I wanted to have it, I desired it with all my might, as if it were the solution to all my trials and tribulations. And I was also very snobbish: Talent seemed something small to me, a petty, unrefined skill that could be honed with the painstaking dedication of artisans and workmen, a vile trade, while my arrogance demanded a true blessing from heaven, a birthright of mine and mine alone that no one could have acquired by mere effort. I wanted to be the chosen one by some divine concession.

And the answer is: I wanted a flame. The image that haunted me was that of a ferocious impulse, an unbearable desire to create, which took hold of me and guided me through the creative process. It wasn't that I cared so much about the genius itself but rather about the lifestyle I imagined it entailed, the urge to wake up every morning and write, or to not be able to go to sleep because my hand wouldn't stop, and to have a thriving and constantly growing connection with the world of ideas and to love those ideas that came to me. I wanted to feel alive and have a mission that justified my existence. I wanted to feel important.

Some people are naturally more gifted than others—that goes without saying. I have always been impressed by the myth of Raphael, who was jealous of Michelangelo; he sneaked into the Sistine Chapel to peek at the work in progress and came out crying. Even at that level, one felt less than the other. And how about Henry Miller, who spent a lifetime trying to become Dostoevsky? Fortunately, he eventually became Henry Miller.

We all come with different gifts and backgrounds, and it's not a variable we can control. Some children pick up a pencil for the first time and can already draw perfect figures. But who said a great artist has to be able to draw well?!

I think the core of the whole issue is something other than that: We wish someone up there had chosen us because we don't have the courage to choose ourselves, to say, "Yes, I am a writer." "Yes, I am a creative." "Yes, I am . . . and I give myself permission to be one."

We need a reason to feel special because we don't know how to believe that we already are special and unique.

Breakdown no. 4

We do not have to ask anyone's permission.

We have to give it to ourselves, and that's where true rebellion lies, in the permission to exist as we are: strange, bizarre, or even the opposite, ordinary, bigoted, in line with the times.

We feel that there is already a genius within us, a demon or daimon, a spirit that guides us and has no need to be perfect; it just needs to be expressed and not dismissed.

5) *Ubi maior?*

One of the most demeaning concepts is *ubi maior minor cessat* (in the presence of a more important person, the less important one loses relevance), a notion that comes to life, for example, in the inalienable maxims that are passed on through generations until it reaches a mother's lips who will say to her child, "It must be true because the teacher said so."

When I was eighteen years old, I was sure that a university design course would turn one into a designer; that the Polytechnic University of Milan was the peak of creativity; that teachers were always prepared and knowledgeable; that ad agencies were a perfect environment to express yourself; that creative directors must have been phenomenal at their jobs.

In short, I was convinced of a lot of bullshit. I had a reverential fear of institutions and hearsay. I harbored a terrible sense of inferiority and thought that everyone was better than me. Consequently, the graduates from that university must be the most qualified, along with those who work for famous brands and those who work for huge companies.

My professional career has seen a long list of disappointments. All the myths I held, which kept me small while giving me comfort (it's convenient for us to think that the teacher is always right because they become a point of reference), turned out to be much more insignificant than I had ever imagined.

I found out that college doesn't really prepare you and there wasn't that much creativity at Milan Polytechnic. When I went to work at Leo Burnett, I saw that even in the famous agency, people could get very frustrated while taking comfort in the thought of being in the big leagues and dealing with high-profile brands (I did the same!). I went to work for One-Plus in China to coordinate two teams, and I discovered that big companies often turn out to be worse than city council offices. I spoke to all sorts of professionals to realize that you can call yourself "creative director" and not be much of a creative director.

I held the myth of the big agency, the big clients, the big company, and the big brands: senior art director, creative director, head of UX, and blah, blah, blah. And I realized that all that glitters ain't gold.

That is why I always advise my students to have as many experiences as possible, to question everything that they're told (even what I say in class), to test it, to see if it works, to see if it makes sense to them. Because *ubi maior* is not always valid. Maybe the right path for them, or for that project, or for that specific situation, is another one.

In the end we have to realize that the only direction we can follow is our own: what we like and what we don't like, what suits us and what doesn't suit us depending on our values and preferences. And if we make a mistake, good for us we have learned something!

Publishing with Penguin is not necessarily good for us; a senior art director working at Google might not be suitable for our company; the author of a best-selling manual on creativity might not be the right consultant for our project.

We have to go beyond hearsay so that we can find environments and people similar to us. If I read *Railroads of Mexico* (Laurana Publisher), which, despite all the positive reviews, I feel lacks soul, then it is not a good book; it is beautifully written, but it is not a good book. If I pick up the IDEO Method Cards, a highly praised product developed by one of the most famous design agencies in the world, I don't feel like

I'm in front of something enlightening; to me it is a poorly functional tool, a useful list of methods but . . . that's about it. When I talked to the social media manager of one of the largest agencies in Turin, she said, "No, you can't just do paid ads on Instagram; you also have to invest in the organic growth otherwise it doesn't work," I gathered that I was standing in front of a great and highly recognized professional, who, outside of her field, could only spew stupidity. It is not a matter of being right; we don't have to care about being right since my opinion only applies to me. For so many people *Railroads of Mexico* is a masterpiece, IDEO Method Cards are phenomenal, and the social media manager in question is the best in her field. That's fine, according to their experience; they are right. The important thing is not to agree with hearsay and labels, but to have the experience ourselves.

And to do so, we need to start by defining our filters.

What do we like? Why? What is important to us? Do we want a product to sell, to be useful, to be environmentally friendly, to be ethical? And what is ethical for us? I find the dream cards published by Gribaudo an insult, because they are not very useful, nothing more than a giftable. To me, the usefulness of a tool is a form of respect for the users. I find Rory's Story Cube a brilliant yet dull product, very easy to use, but after three times, you can put it in a corner and forget about it. For me, continuity in use and universality of a tool are crucial.

And for you? What is important?

Breakdown no. 5

Let's decide to break all conditioning from myths, labels, and authoritative ideas.

Let's take back our freedom to raise our heads, to form our own opinions, and to find what works for us. Even at the risk of appearing arrogant and thinking or talking nonsense.

Let's have the courage to have an opinion and state it. We are not wrong because we think differently from others.

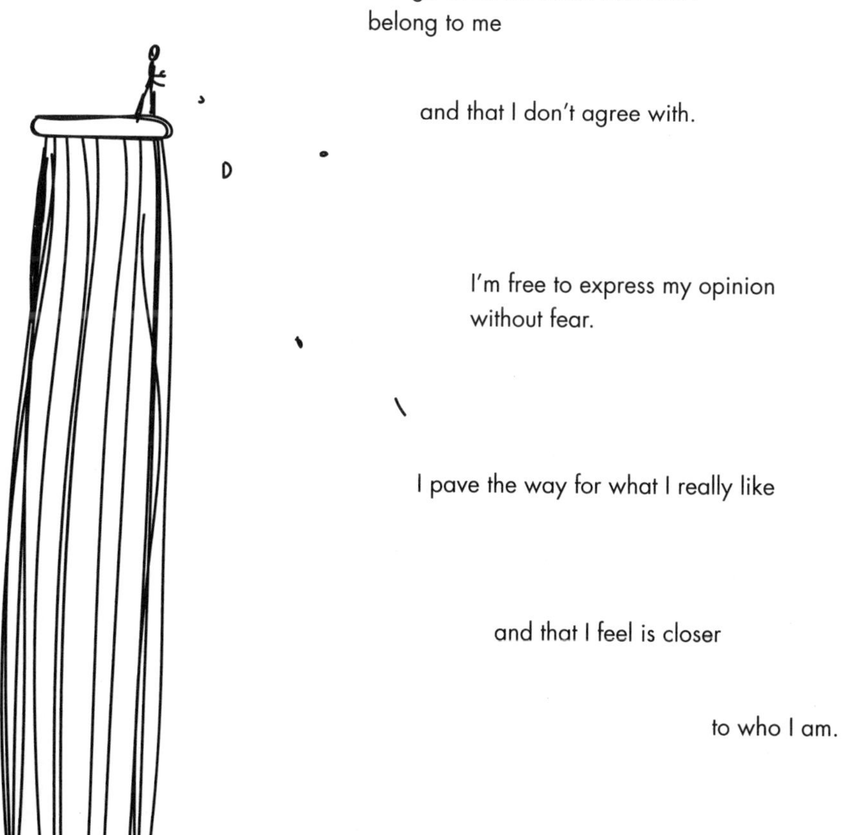

6) Creativity is not only enthusiasm

There is a tendency to imagine creativity as an unbridled party of joy, an inexhaustible source that flows from the hands and goes on its own, possessing the half-spiked creative person who switches to autopilot. A bit like what happens on social media when people only post pics in which they look happy and fulfilled; same goes with the creative process which becomes the "right one" when we are happy, cheerful, open, energetic, "functional." And this positive, perfect, illusory imagery is likely to make us feel wrong when the opposite happens.

Creativity is not a perfect process. All creative people struggle, at any level. The more they engage in some self-criticism, the more they demand of themselves. They don't just put out the first thing that comes to mind, but they work on it again and again, always keeping in mind that what will come out is not necessarily good. It is *also* joy, heroic fury, madness, wonder. That too. But there is also despair—wandering without a path, feeling like we are worthless while the magnitude of something that hasn't come out yet weighs us down.

Bottom line: It's not a fairy tale. This is what we have to go through to want to be creative: to have the courage to feel like crap while we confront our own limits.

We shouldn't be afraid to come down to earth, to feel inadequate, naive, unprepared, miserable, incapable, inattentive, lazy, clumsy, and the list goes on and on.

We can also feel like that. We need to learn how to deal with it, because it'll often be like this. We will be tempted to run and hide with our tails between our legs thinking, "This is horrible, just horrible. I came up with pure shit, I'm worthless." It's okay. Laugh it out. It happens to the best of us, it's part of the game. There is no perfect world and no perfect way. We all scratch our noses and poop; the greatest of writers can wrinkle their noses and out of the blue let out a resounding fart. Ha ha. Let's enjoy the ups and downs, while letting go of what is ideal and of how we think we *should* be. Let's allow ourselves to be human: It's much more fun.

We have to have the courage to feel small and put up with it, to grow up, to be seized by the doubt that makes us think that we don't know how to write as well we would like, paint as well as we would like, invent as well as we would like, and that what we created is not good enough.

It happens to me a lot. Yesterday I reread a manuscript I had to turn in to my editor, and I sulked all day. Because I knew something's wrong, I knew I didn't get as far as I wanted to go, and it made me sulk—I was tempted to lock myself in the house and burn everything down.

This is the energy, the intensity I'm talking about. I'm not going to back down, thinking, "I'm a loser 'cause I shouldn't feel like this." Enough of that!

Who decides how a creative person should feel? Who said that failure is really a failure? Remember that there is light and there is darkness. And we must learn to want to stay in the dark. We can't settle, rather we must be willing to feel unworthy at times, to have the courage to approach the desk and get our hands back on a manuscript, a painting or any other kind of project.

Come on, it's not that hard!

Breakdown no. 6

Let's take note that there is no one-size-fits-all model for how to be creative. There will be sunny days and rainy days, there will be screaming and crying, and most importantly there will be what is right for us, depending on our age, the moment we're living, and the project we're working on.

Next time someone asks us, "How are you?" try to be truthful. Whether you're talking to an acquaintance at the bar or with your mom who calls you before dinner time.

If we felt miserable that day, admit it, "I'm not good, I don't like what I wrote today." "Horrible. I couldn't take one step forward with the project." "I feel like shit. I felt like someone who couldn't even hold a brush in his hand."

Dare to be yourself and enjoy the responses of those who often fill us with fear. Someone will look at you in amazement as if to say, "I thought you were supposed to be creative!" Someone else might offer an empathetic smile.

So? Do we really need to be scared? Or did we already manage to overcome the idea of perfection that someone had embedded in our soul? If we are willing to endure falling flat on our asses and admit it, we can do whatever we want.

We are free.

7) Those who have more ideas are not necessarily the most creative

We often get the impression that Gregory is an extremely creative person as he talks about his ideas for an app, an innovative restaurant, a medical service, another app, a business abroad, a fast food restaurant, etc. We have been convinced that being a nonstop gushing fountain is synonymous with creativity: If you have a lot of ideas, you are creative. It's an American-style capitalistic concept: The more, the better.

The obvious consequence is that, if we are not constantly churning out ideas, we feel inferior.

But let's take a good look at Gregory. We all know a Gregory or Allison. They laugh, joke around, and enjoy themselves while they talk about their latest idea. But in the end . . . have they ever finalized one? Have they ever taken action? Or do they simply have fun (and at the same time they dread) pestering us? But mostly: How valid are those ideas? Are they grounded, feasible, or are they just plain ridiculous? There are some Gregorys who will walk up to us and say, "I had an incredible idea, I'll give it to you since I will never carry it out." Ha ha. So why should I do it?

It happens to me a lot with Sefirot. Dozens of Gregorys write to me: "I had an idea! Let's make a Fabula for chefs," "A Fabula for musicians," "A Fabula for woodworkers." And when I say, "Okay, sounds intriguing, how do you plan on doing it?" they say, "I don't know. I gave you the idea, you worry about the rest, but I want a percentage on sales!" That really puts my nose out of joint.

But there is an even lower level, and that's when Gregory is more structured and his idea is a bit more outlined. Usually when a project is pitched to me, I ask the submitter to fill out a short presentation sheet (that I created ad hoc to help me skim the projects), and in 80 percent of the cases the answer I get is: "Can't we hop on a call? I don't have time to waste." They don't have time to invest in their own ideas, yet I should find time to listen to them. Funny, right?

Having lots of unrealized, or unachievable, ideas is not being creative—it is just making a huge mess. Not to mention the time and energy we are asked to waste on their ideas. Gregorys are overachievers and at worst leeches who suck the most important lymph from us: wholeness. They make us feel fragmented and eroded by the wind.

We must remember what the basic requirement of creativity is. True creative people create, do, accomplish. The ideas they have are good enough (or at least, they believe they are) to excite them and produce the urge to work on them. It is an unmistakable feeling, because out of the blue, we feel a push to take action.

A few months after Sefirot opened, my partner and I realized that we could come up with a hundred ideas an hour: tools for branding, advertising, marketing, project management, strategy, learning a language, for essay writing, for training at home (and I could go on for another ten pages). So we set out to create an in-between place for these ideas, the box-of-ideas-in-waiting.

The box-of-ideas-in-waiting would host all the projects we didn't feel like working on at the time, knowing that sooner or later something in there would ripen and come knocking. Fabula for Kids, for example, was in the box for two years. Edito for four.

We are not creative because of the number of ideas we cram in our box, but because of the ones we have the desire to bring to life.

Breakdown no. 7

We are not factories. Let's break away (now! immediately!) from the concept that quantity is always synonymous with abundance. Our creative abundance is not quantifiable. Let's decide to stop allowing the Gregorys in our lives to make us feel less than worthy.

We are not less than anyone.

The only person to which we owe something is ourselves.

I'm sure that the right ideas will come at the right time.

My will to create tends toward infinity
and I'm ready to let it capture me
and shake me.

8) Creativity cannot be taught

We have Lucy who decided to join a writing class; Jason who studies graphics at university; Carmelo who has been studying with a master painter for five years; Freddy who works at night to pay for a degree in art direction and copywriting.

Lucy might learn how to write well; Jason to be a graphic designer; Carmelo to paint; Freddy to understand and apply with rigor and efficiency the mechanisms of communication. They can learn the technicalities, they can become good professionals, but no one can teach them how to be creative.

It is one thing to know how to paint a vase with flowers, another to feel that the vase is calling us, and that for some obscure reason, we have the urge and duty to put it on a canvas. It is one thing to know how to create an advertising campaign, quite another to have an epiphany while grocery shopping and having to stop on a bench to jot down an idea before it disappears.

Creativity is self-expression, even the part of us that we do not perceive, the most intimate, hidden, nocturnal self. It is like a hammer striking a cord hundreds of miles into the earth and producing vibrations that run all the way up to the other end of the cord, where a note finally comes out. It is not enough to know how to do it: It takes the string, the hammer, and the will to vibrate and let ourselves be shocked by it.

You cannot teach this, you can only inspire it. I can tell you about my own experience and that of the people I have met in the hopes that something resonates with you, and it makes you say, "Oh, so it can be done!," "I'm not alone," or even something deeper: "Yes, yes, yes! This is good! This is exactly it!" Something that will push you to explore your own self on another level, to open up and let out what you really want to give to the world and to yourself.

Let's start!

Grab a piece of paper and do something that establishes and reinforces your will. Write:

> I am a creative spirit.
> I have no patterns and no limits.
> I want to expand and break out into this world.

Fold this piece of paper, put it under your pillow, in your jacket pocket, in your desk drawer. Let it work.

And let the magic begin.

PART II

To Awaken

Looking inward

Rocking the world is the easy part. It is not so challenging to pick up the pliers and tear off the staples with which the scenography around us is set. The judgment and heroic fury of destroying external agents, of dismantling, are actions we are used to. These actions make you feel satisfied and relieved. We can look at the rubble of the receding city and think, "There, it wasn't me. It was her fault. It was him. It was the environment. It was the rules set by who knows who."

This is the first step, the one that frees us from limits, that allows us to walk in a place where we can build what we want, following our own will without having to compromise with anyone.

But in this new scenario, where we are the first dot on a blank page, there is still one super impactful problem: us.

We have to awaken, see the limits we have introjected from the outside or even the brand-new ones we created because we were scared of failure, success, growing up, love, or a deep distrust of everything and everyone. We must dismantle ourselves, our mechanisms, our structures, our masks.

And I can guarantee that this is way more painful.

You will find out that it was easier to blame the world. Ha ha.

The most terrifying aspect about creativity

When I was nineteen years old, I attended the design school in Genoa, which was part of the school of architecture, and there I received one of the most severe emotional beatings of my life.

It was my first assignment of the year. We worked in a group of three to submit the first draft of a graphic design project. I don't even remember what it was; it's not important. What I do remember vividly was the teacher's feedback. He looked at our boards with disgust painted on his face, and he proceeded to say, "It's not good." At that time I was young, arrogant, and full of myself, so I clenched my fists and said to him, "What part is not good?" But he didn't really tell me. He said that everything was wrong, he didn't like it, it didn't pertain to the brief he gave us. Bottom line, we had to redo the whole thing.

My schoolmates smoked a cigarette and left campus mumbling. I, on the other hand, remained leaning against one of the building's balustrades for at least three hours, until it became dark. What had happened had shocked me.

I was used to being good at math in school, I solved a problem, and no one could object. Instead, now I felt the earth trembling beneath my feet.

There was no logic. The professor was probably right, yet even he couldn't explain exactly why. I looked at the boards again. Yes, something didn't add up. It was subjective, and subjectivity is unpredictable. I felt that I should somehow connect to another level that seemed ephemeral and unattainable at that moment, and it took my breath away.

It was clear to me that I was entering a world without fixed rules, where I would have no inner grips, no formulas or safety nets, no fixed paths. Nor was I going to find any excuses.

I put the boards against the wall and studied them again.

I didn't like them either, but—damn—I couldn't say why.

I learned in that moment the most important lesson of my creative life: Creativity is subjective and unpredictable. So later in life, when my creative director told me the fateful sentence: "Make it less New York and more San Francisco," I knew what he meant. The same goes with other comments like "More premium," "Less Apple," "It's too childish," "It's too clean." I would no longer relate to thoughts but to the emotions and impressions that the images were able to convey, and I would also learn that subjectivities can clash, that I could convince my boss and clients that my perception was better than theirs, and I did not necessarily need to have a reason.

I was wandering in uncharted territory that was impossible to map, an infinite and limitless ocean, and I was this tiny little guy on top of a little boat having to accept that I was at the mercy of something huge and majestic that could not be bent, persuaded, or forced, but only welcomed, listened to, and cruised.

And that would never change. There will never be a way out of this discomfort; there will never be dry land, because that midnight-blue ocean below, deep and full of monsters and treasures, is an expression of us. That's the state in which the creative exists, the terror of being overturned by our own selves—now the sun is shining, a moment later there is a storm, and the task is learning to laugh at the waves and cry when it's calm again—while we know deep inside that there is nothing worse than landing on an island and not wanting to to set sail again.

When we unhinge dogmas, as we did in the first part of this book, we realize that we found them useful. It was very comfortable to think that we could keep creativity at bay, that we could shine in the Milan Polytechnic, that an art director's designation would make us feel safe, that we could learn a framework or lateral thinking to get out of whatever problem. We realize they were funnels for something immeasurable, and now that we no longer have them, we have to deal with this greatness that we have access to.

We also realize that if we fail to draw from that immensity, we are the ones to blame: We are the malfunctioning funnels.

Inner blocks

The following bullet points are the most common issues I have encountered both in me and in friends, colleagues, and acquaintances, and they serve to wake us up, to put us up against the wall, under scrutiny, to blow off the arrogance and excuses, to help us see where we are lacking and why.

1) I don't feel creative enough

A coworker and friend of mine came to me, sad and hunched over, and she told me that she didn't feel creative enough. She said this as she groveled, feeling sorry for herself and for me since I was the one paying her salary at the time. The first temptation was to put my hand on her shoulder and say, "Poor child, what's wrong? Where did you get stuck?" Basically, I wanted to feel sorry for her. Thankfully, I stopped myself from being paternalistic. I withdrew my hand and told her, "If you don't feel creative enough, it means you're not." She didn't fall apart: She knew that already. She blinked a couple of times, then she stopped playing the victim and nooded.

If we do not feel creative enough, it means at that moment, we are not creative.

We can only fool ourselves to a certain extent. If I write a story without momentum, throwing words on the page without even rereading it and have almost no pleasure in having done so, I know I wasn't very creative. I simply know that! If I don't feel like working and do as little as possible, I know I am not being creative.

When I was designing intùiti's brand, I was dealing with my first personal project (I was twenty-three years old), and my teacher told me, "It's clear that you just threw it together. How many drafts have you done? How much time did you spend on the font? How many times have you looked at it, then thrown everything away and started again?" And I knew it: I knew I had just gone with the first idea, developed it hastily, and slapped it onto the package. There wasn't a second or third version—just one. Arrogant, poorly executed, and even I looked at it with doubt.

When I acknowledged my boastfulness, I went home and produced dozens and dozens of different versions. At first I felt angry and rebellious, I wanted to tell my teacher, "I'll show you," but little by little, I entered another dimension. I would put five fonts next to each other and compare them, and I wasn't doing it to do the homework or because "it had to be done that way" or because I was following a methodology. I did it because I *wanted* to find intùiti's font, and I felt a visceral need to find out which one it was. At one point I told myself it was going to be Centennial; however, I didn't like the *u*. My teacher once again came to the rescue telling me that a font can be picked apart; I could tear it, turn it, and I thought, "Why not?" So I took the *n* and I flipped it into a *u*. And I started liking it. I went on for days and nights testing, studying, and asking friends and colleagues to give me their opinions. Making the intùiti brand had become a joyful endeavor. When I finished and laid out what is still on the package today, I was finally satisfied. I was proud of the result, ready to defend it tooth and nail, and I knew I had been creative for a few days.

From then on, I could always recognize whether I had been creative enough or not. After feeling the thrill of excitement, the need to really put myself into something, I no longer had any doubts: If I don't feel that way, I'm not really creative. And it makes no sense for me to whine and bug myself, or others, with the story of my not being enough: When we realize what works, we have to take responsibility for it. If we don't feel that we are creative enough, we need to understand why and, if we want to be creative, act instead of making excuses.

Awakening no. 1

Let's ask:

- When was the last time I didn't feel creative enough?
- And the last time I truly felt creative?

We can write down the answers in a notebook that we will use throughout our journey, so we can go back and see how our perception will change over time.

Let's try to go back to the feeling we had when we felt really creative. Close your eyes, breathe in the scents, taste the flavors, and remember the energy you felt. What is the image you see? When this happens to me, for example, I get this loud and slightly unusual laugh. We treasure that vibration so we can recognize it when it happens again: We were able to be creative, and we felt it. Every time we don't feel that way, there is no question about it: We are not as creative as we could have been!

Now let's talk about the most uncomfortable part: How come we didn't feel creative enough? Let's do some soul-searching:

What was our advantage in not being creative? Laziness? Did we not care about the project? Did we feel bored? Let's try writing down three or four reasons, then ask ourselves if they are good enough reasons for doing things half-heartedly, tepidly. We can also accept that the important thing is taking responsibility for the way we are or are not creative (also because complaining is a super noncreative attitude, ha ha).

Frequently asked question: How do we know if we have not been creative enough?

If there is no pride in the result, we most likely were not. It also happens when cooking: If I've made spaghetti with clams the way I like, which I've tried time and time again and in which I've put effort and love, and someone tells me the dish is not that great, I'll smash the plate on their heads. I'm proud of my pasta, and I'm ready to defend it. Even if it wasn't outstanding, I would stand by it, and that's what matters.

2) Blocks are not where we think they are

The myth of the blank page exists: I want to create something, but that something does not come. I stare at the screen or the page and don't feel like writing, or I start doing it and throw it away because it doesn't nurture me.

Sofia wants to write a book, but she is stuck on chapter five and can't move forward. Daniel is bored at work, and he needs to come up with ideas but feels like an empty tube of toothpaste. Phil knows that his company is not performing as he would like, yet he cannot get out of the routine, the repetition, of his daily tasks. He has no energy to find an alternative solution.

These are recurring scenarios, in which we have all found ourselves or will find ourselves at some point. When this happens, we generally tend to feel bad for a time and finally react with a major burst of energy: Sofia forces herself into the chair and writes and rewrites the same chapter till she drops, hoping that the creative juices will start flowing again; Daniel struggles during a brainstorming session and then picks the two ideas that are acceptable within the bunch; Phil works night and day to turn the company's fate around, very often going in the wrong direction. The reaction we are tempted to have is raging, a dying animal holding on to life, trying everything and unfortunately facing the wrong enemy.

The plant is not bearing fruit and we try to keep it alive by putting sticks around it; we don't worry about the aquifer that has dried up a few miles upstream. We look at the most obvious symptom instead of going deeper, to the root of the issue.

In 2023, while working full-time at Sefirot, I felt a great sense of discouragement: I was supposed to develop more creative tools (at least that's what I told myself), but I didn't have the drive. I tried putting down dozens of ideas—a product for dreams, for branding, for bioenergetics, for art direction, for marketing, for prompt engineering, I even thought about doing an intùiti 2.0—and I felt no pleasure in the thought of actually developing any of them. I didn't have the drive, and I realized what would happen if I simply made an effort: I would spend energy and effort to develop a mediocre product. This is precisely the most frequent result: By acting out of frustration, we put together something that we are not proud of, that does not nourish us, and in fact, gnaws at us from the inside.

A few months later, during a trip to San Francisco, I discovered that my partner, with whom I founded the company, was judging my irrational side, my nonconventional choices, my outbursts of madness (the very ones that had made Sefirot great). There was no malice in his judgment—he didn't want to judge me, but he couldn't help himself. And I realized immediately that I could feel him: I felt him as a shadowy presence in every room, a limit I struggled to overcome. We decided to separate professionally, and after the first period of settling in, the momentum flourished again: I felt like embarking on a major challenge, to write a book on creativity—this book—that I would never have started with him by my side, because I felt the unbearable skepticism in his eyes, because I feared there was also envy and I didn't want to show off and break the status quo, because he carried a vibration so different from mine that made flying high impossible.

It was the same for him. He was leading a frustrating life because I was egging him on with my enthusiasm and inciting him to live more dangerously. When I stepped out of the scenario, he went back to doing what he wanted to do: teaching.

In short, we traveled a piece of road together, then I began to limit him, and he began to limit me, like two forces that cannot be too close.

My problem was not finding ideas or laziness; it was the presence of a partner who was simply too different from me.

Maybe Sofia's problem is that she doesn't really want to write that novel; and Daniel can't stand his boss; and Phil's issue is connected to the obligation he has imposed upon himself to work eight hours a day like he would in an office when what he really needs is more freedom.

So where does the real root of creative block lie?

Awakening no. 2

Let's write down the symptom of our block in this form:

I can't . . .

For example: "I can't write a book," "I can't find a new idea," "I can't come up with something new," or "I can't go to work happy in the morning."

Now, let's change "I can't" to "I don't want to" and add a reason why:

I don't want to write the book because . . .

Try to be as unhinged as possible, and think about what your advantage might be in limiting yourself. But careful: The word is not *excuse*. The word is *advantage*. What is in it for you? What do you gain? How come we found a way to screw ourselves, to tie our own hands behind our backs?

- *I don't want to write the book because I don't want to be in competition with my girlfriend who is also a writer.*
- *I don't want to do something I like because I don't want my roommate to feel bad, since he complains about work all day long.*
- *I don't want to find a solution for my company because I don't like people who have too much money, and I don't want to become like them.*

Let's go as deep as we can. Let's climb the rope of *why* until we find the one that will make us scream, "Oh, shit."

You'll see how the pieces will fall into place: Water will go back flowing toward the plant.

I don't want to create new tools because I don't want to unleash my creative potential. I don't want to unleash it because I don't want to show off. I don't want to show off because I don't want to overshadow the person next to me. I don't want to overshadow the person because I don't want them to make me pay for it.

I don't want to invent new products because I don't feel safe.

3) Complaining is not creative

For a year and a half, I've opened my house on Wednesdays to friends and strangers for group sessions with intùiti where we use the cards to work on creative blocks. Usually one of the most popular issues that newcomers raise is related to dissatisfaction at work, which leads to other kinds of problems (constipation, anxiety, panic, stomach aches, migraines, etc.). When I worked at Leo Burnett, I developed stress vertigo that stuck to me for ten very long months, even after I quit my job. I used to walk back home from work holding on to the wall, which was zero fun.

What amazes me the most about this issue is the level of endurance that some people manage to achieve: years of physical symptoms and doctor visits, even major ones—colonoscopies for intestinal blockages, heart palpitations, Holter monitors, etc.—without ever considering quitting, leaving, changing jobs, or taking a break.

What happens very often is that after an intùiti session, having realized that their job is killing them, they absolutely do not even want to consider quitting. They come up with excuses. I don't like it but . . . Yes, it's true, it's killing me, and yet in the past few days . . . Come on, it's not so bad after all . . .

Complaining is our way of holding up a situation; we invest energy in the act of talking about it so we can endure longer. We vent and that makes us feel temporarily better, heard, understood, and seen. When I worked at Leo Burnett, we all seemed to be victims of a collective trauma: We couldn't wait to see each other at happy hour to complain. Every once in a while someone would say, "Let's stop talking about work," but it never happened: There was nothing else we wanted to talk about, and the only topic we cared about was the terrible experience that was scarring our lives. And we gloated like staisfied pigs as we vomited painful words. Somehow it compensated for all the discomfort we had inside.

The problem lies in repetition: The whining always sounds the same. It goes on endlessly, and there is never a creative attitude, a break that marks the beginning of a new era.

I know people who have been complaining about the same thing, about work or a colleague or a partner, saying the same things for more than five years, yet they do nothing to change their situation. And clearly the complaining becomes an energy black hole, so it is almost impossible for them to feel creative.

What's the point of going to the same restaurant every day, where we know we're not going to eat well? We go, we eat, we pay, and then we complain when we get home. We had a bad meal, and we spent the evening complaining. Wouldn't it be better to change the restaurant?

Someone will say, "But what if I'm afraid to change? But what if I can't afford it?" What if, what if, what if. No matter how abundant and well-constructed the excuses are, they will not be able to erase the reality of your situation: Every time we complain, there is something limiting us that we are not facing.

Complaining is an important symptom that needs to be treated with care and brought to the surface. How long have I been complaining about my job, my friend, my girlfriend, my boss, my colleague? And how come I don't do anything about it?

If Lucy comes to intùiti readings and complains about her job and, by going deeper, it becomes clear that it would be very good for her to quit, at the next reading Lucy cannot come back and say the same things she said the time before, because she will get the same answer—again and again. If she does not want to change her job, or her attitude about it, why continue? What's in it for her?

In short, we have to ask ourselves what is our benefit in being in a situation we don't like.

I used to complain about the agency, but I put up with it because I wanted to build a solid résumé. I got stress vertigo because I wanted to work for big brands. I wanted people to look at my LinkedIn page and say, "Wow, he's good."

Lucy says that her company is full of unprofessional people who don't know how to work, and maybe that's why she wants to work there: to feel better than everyone else.

The problem is not the complaining itself but not knowing why we are handling something we don't like so poorly. No one is forcing us to do it. There's no medal for suffering.

If I'm working in a place I hate because I need the money, because I have a family to support and I can't afford to quit the job out of the blue, my benefit is money. And there is nothing wrong with that. Once I know my benefit, I can put my heart to rest and say to myself, "Matteo, you need this job. Don't sweat it, just look for something else. Once you find something else, you can quit." My attitude, from moaning at the bar to actively looking for a new job, has already changed.

Awakening no. 3

Write a list of the things or people we have complained about in the past few months.

For example:

- *My boss.*
- *My job.*
- *My house.*
- *My lack of free time.*
- *My colleague.*

Then let's ask ourselves how much we have complained about it from one to ten, where one is *just a little* and ten is *constantly*, and then mark the level of complaint next to each item.

Now let's think of a person we know who is always complaining, the complainer par excellence, who tells us the same things over and over and, if we try to tell them to do something about it, the answer is always: "It's easy for you to say." You can even write more than one name.

- *Daniel.*

Perfect. Let's take a good look at the name written on the sheet. Let's remember feeling powerless trying to get Daniel to stop whining, and even how much we hate hearing the same stuff over and over again.

We are like Daniel.

Same, same. Ha ha. Our friends won't tell us, out of kindness, out of politeness, but we have been boring them with our complaints the same way Daniel does with us.

So, since—I don't know about you—but I hate feeling unbearable, let's try working on our complaints.

What do we gain from putting up with that situation?

- *My boss—I don't want to be confrontational; I get nervous just thinking about it.*
- *My job—I like the safety it gives me, in another place maybe I would be asked to work harder.*
- *My house—is cheap.*
- *My lack of free time—if I had more time, then I would have to dedicate it to writing the book I have been talking about for a long time. And the thought terrifies me.*
- *My colleague—same as my boss, I don't want to get into it.*

For which of these is the advantage truly insignificant compared to the discomfort we feel?

It could be all of them—or none at all.

Now close your eyes and imagine having solved all the issues on your list, one by one. I'm on good terms with my boss: How do I feel? I changed jobs: How am I doing? How am I dressed? Do I like my colleagues? Am I smiling? I live in a new house: Do I like it?

And here we are, imagining the world as we would like it to be: Look at us being creative.

4) I don't know what I want to do

When we finally admit that we don't want to do what we are doing, we are left wondering, "What is it that I want to do? What do I like?" Perhaps one of the advantages we had for not quitting was exactly not having to deal with those questions. Because not knowing what we like feels like a terrifying black hole. On one side, there are those people who wanted to be doctors knowing that's what they loved—they do it and wow, good for them; on the other side, there are those who have been saying the same thing forever, "I don't know what I want to do when I grow up."

Peter is thirty-four years old. He tells me that work is killing him, that he hasn't liked what he does in years, that he suffers from acid reflux. When I ask him what he would like to do instead of working the job he's stuck with now, he says, "I have no idea." When I ask him what he liked to do when he was little, what his dreams were, he answers, "I don't remember."

More often than we think, we forget what we wanted to do. We lose what Hillman calls "the acorn" in his *The Soul's Code*, the seed that is already visible in children, our most intimate essence that tells us who we want to be when we grow up. Those who want to be doctors don't forget it, because it is a job well accepted by society; it happens to those who wanted to be painters, chefs, carpenters, writers, artists, and when parents would have preferred for their kid to be an engineer or a lawyer.

That's why Peter, as much as I keep on asking, "How in the hell can you not remember what you wanted to be when you grew up?," looks lost to me, sad even, for not having an answer.

My acorn was pretty clear from the start: When I was eight years old, I would sit in front of my grandmother's typewriter and pretend to write a new *Don Quixote*. Not just that—when I was seven, I begged my mom to buy me a tarot deck along with the manual at the local general store. It was published by Edizioni Demetra, and I still remember since I studied that deck word by word. I wanted to be a writer, and more broadly, I wanted to be creative—and of course, my inclination for the esoteric (and for cards) was already rooted inside of me. It was obvious that I was going to open a company like Sefirot, right? Connect the dots, draw a line, it is simple.

But how long did it take me to remember?

Years. Long years spent punching myself on the head while feeling like a failure and ungrateful because I was never happy. I worked in agencies and didn't like it, in corporations and didn't like it, as a freelancer and didn't like it. Art direction, UX, advertising, none of it mattered; I was missing the real yearning. I understand well how Peter feels. I, too, felt lost and craved literary genius; however, I didn't allow myself to even imagine leading the life of a writer. The feeling that comes from this MO is one of helplessness; you want to fall on a bench and say, "I don't know what to do with my life."

Why couldn't I see the signs? There were many. At twenty-five, I told my boss in Amsterdam, "What I would love is to open a publishing house." I couldn't stop creating new products and the card format was somehow haunting me; I always went back to that, to the point that one day, as I walked to the agency, I had the idea—I can open a publishing house that specializes in tools for creativity!—but the image fled. And what was the height of my career as a UX designer? Writing a book about it. Ha ha. I mean, can it get clearer than this?

I didn't want to see the signs because they all sounded like unrealizable dreams. A publishing house? You're nuts! On top of that, a publishing house that only sells tools for creativity? Come on man, it's impossible! Oh, and you want to be a writer . . . that's a good one.

We don't forget about our dreams because we are forgetful. It happens because we don't allow ourselves to dream. We erase the signs of what we wanted to do, and that amazing muscle called "I want" becomes atrophied—we don't know how to want, so we end up not wanting anything anymore.

There is an unforgettable sentence in Italian that our parents love to repeat, and it goes: "The 'I Want' grass doesn't even grow in the King's garden," which basically means you can't always get what you want. This saying should be banned.

What we must do is precisely take the "I Want" grass.

Awakening no. 4

Let's write what we want to do, what we like. Not necessarily the job we want; there's always time to turn the dream into work.

For example:

- *Read.*
- *Write.*
- *Run.*
- *Take walks.*
- *Talk about books and films.*

And try to focus on remembering details about our lives when we were little, when we played with friends outdoors, when we liked certain things to the point of almost being obsessed with them. Give yourself permission to remember. What did you love? Call your parents if you want and ask them—they might give you some interesting hints. If you can, write what age you were next to each entry.

- *I used to sneak into my neighbor's workshop, and I built toys with pieces of wood. I was three years old.*
- *I was obsessed with vampires. It started when I was nine.*
- *My dad would tell me stories, and I would tell them to my kindergarten classmates, adding or changing details. I was five years old.*
- *I read tarot cards to my elementary school teacher. She got scared because I guessed an event from her past; she forbade me to bring the cards to school again. I was eight years old.*
- *I asked my IT teacher how viruses were created. She replied that "they are born out of nowhere." I didn't believe her; I persevered and learned how to program to make viruses. I was twelve years old.*
- *I won a contest for a logo design. I was thirteen years old.*

Are there any threads that we can grab and pull? Is there any leitmotif that stands out? From the notes I sense a creative, rebellious, and somewhat impatient child who loves stories and the world of magic.

Who is this child that we are not allowing ourselves to be?

5) To feel turned off

When I was twenty-seven, I spent a month going to work, coming home, and watching *The Walking Dead,* the series about zombies. That's all I did: work and TV. I felt exhausted; I would wake up in the morning, and no matter how much I slept, I felt depressed and weak. I would tell myself that I was working a lot and that the kind of work I was doing was stressful; however, the truth was that an eerie silence lived inside of me. My real voice would not come out. So I would sit in front of the screen and let fictional characters live instead of me: They would speak, feel emotions, be afraid, run away. Even external inputs had a relatively small impact on me. When my girlfriend at the time came to visit, I didn't even feel like going out to dinner or making love; I just wanted to numb myself in front of the TV series. She would get nervous and I would get pissed off. "I just want to relax," I would tell her, "I just want to rest."

Now I know that when we feel dull, tired, worn out in all aspects of our lives—creativity, sex, appetite—we are facing a pretty serious symptom.

We tell ourselves that we are just tired, that we have done a lot and need to take a break, but that break could last for years.

Sonia, a former coworker of mine, tells me that she spent a week doing nothing and now feels more tired than before. Lucy would like to change jobs but doesn't have the strength in the evening to open LinkedIn and update her résumé. Carlo tells me the same story. And so do Gregory and Phil. They will do it later, as soon as they feel more . . . the right word is *alive*, but they don't say it. They don't dare. They prefer using *rested.*

I learned the difference between fatigue and intensity when I told my teacher, "I'm writing in the evenings and working during the day. It's tiring," and she said, "Careful. If it's tiring, there's something wrong with it. Otherwise it is *intense.*"

When the work is intense, you can tell because it generates energy. One thing is to spend an amazing evening, having the time of your life, and the next morning you lie devastated in bed, smiling because the exhaustion you feel is a good one; it is the result of a healthy and happy outlet. Another thing is to wake up and want to curl up because you feel that life is slipping through your fingers, and you're doing nothing to prevent it from happening.

When I was working on intùiti's Kickstarter campaign in February 2013, I slept two or three hours a day for about a month. I looked exhausted. The barista at my favorite coffee shop used to tell me that I looked like a skeleton, yet, despite the obvious physical and mental strain, I felt electric, vibrant, strong, and happy. It was nothing like the next experience, when I worked half the time and was basically depressed.

This is the core of it all. Let's pay attention to the difference between tiredness and depression. In the first instance, we jump into bed, we sleep like babies, and we wake up feeling new. In the second case, we exist inside some sort of nightmare: We notice because we don't really want to do anything—neither read a book nor run or go for a walk, nor make love. We do everything by dragging our bodies and then seeking solace in brain-eating routines, such as social media, Netflix, and so on.

When we are depressed, we are repressing something. Maybe we have realized that our job is shit, that the book we are writing is shit, that our love story is shit, and that we are shit because we don't succeed, because we are not good enough or passionate enough, and instead of saying it and admitting it out loud, we repress it so the energy doesn't flow.

How can we be creative if we suppress what we really feel? I came out of that little depression when my relationship ended, and I admitted that the experience with the big agency had turned out to be an overwhelming disappointment.

Years later, it happened again. I shut myself off for six months: Without even realizing it, I avoided continuing with *Mario*, my series of novels, because I was afraid my girlfriend would get angry. I was right: When I wrote that book, she lost it. A friend of mine did the same; he didn't write poetry because he didn't want his wife to notice that he loved the shadow of a street sign more than he loved her. And how many of us don't do something or say something for fear of the consequences?

But how can we live without that intensity, without screaming, without confrontation, without tears?

When I gave the novel to my girlfriend, I left the house and my legs were shaking. I was gone all night, and when I returned we had a fight.

At least I felt alive.

Awakening no. 5

Are there aspects of our lives or our days that make us feel tired? Let's try to pinpoint them.

Write them down:

- *Talking to the accountant.*
- *Taking care of the business' bureaucratic matters.*
- *Cleaning the house.*

They can also appear to be innocent or fun matters.

For example:

- *Going out with friends for a drink.*

These are all factors that drain us. What are we suppressing about these aspects of our day? What are we hiding? Let's be daring: Let's find a reason, even a remote one, that can make sense.

- *When I talk to my accountant or I deal with bureaucratic issues, I get headaches and my anxiety spikes. I complain with others, I blame the Italian government for being so complicated and cumbersome and yada yada, but in all honesty, I feel like I just don't know about the topic enough. I feel that I am a distracted entrepreneur, a boy who doesn't know what he's doing, and this gives me anxiety and I get angry at myself.*
- *Cleaning the house makes me nervous. I run back and forth between laundry and a business call. I get nervous because it seems that domestic chores rob me of my free time. But is it true? Truth be told, I pile on these things when I want to distract myself, when creativity becomes too much. I use it as a way out.*

What happens when I admit these omissions to myself? First of all, I could study bureaucratic matters that make me anxious so that I could feel like I have everything under control, and, I must say, the idea of learning about budgets, invoices, and other such matters doesn't bother me at all. For the house, I may just call the maid service one more time, and remind myself that if I'm tempted to fuss over the quilt that needs washing, it means that I need to do just the opposite: focus on the work task that is challenging me.

When it comes to friends, it can be a bit more obnoxious. When people around us wear us down, it's because they're always complaining about the same things, or because we don't feel they're aligned with our thinking, or it could be that we're in a new phase of our lives. Maybe I need to hang out with people who are more like me. Maybe I have become too detached from some of my lifelong friends. Maybe we will rekindle later on.

If we repress something, we are not dumb: We usually do it because it would hurt us to admit the truth. Unfortunately, we pay the price with our energy . . . and a lot of our creativity goes down the drain too.

6) I can't think of anything

I talk to Samantha, who is very unhappy about becoming an engineer, so I ask her why she studied engineering instead of something else. She gives me a surprised look, as if my question was the most unexpected one in the world, and tells me she doesn't know. "Well, I urge you to think about it now: How come you signed up for something you didn't like?" Without even taking a few seconds to think about it, she immediately replies, "I can't think of anything."

How is it possible that she never asked herself, "How did I end up in this situation?"

I don't know how, but I know that it is indeed possible. The problem is that we don't really care about ourselves that much. We focus on our ambitions, on short-term goals, but we don't dedicate time to ourselves, to our system, to the myriad of reasons why we are the way we are and we aren't the way we would like to be.

We can't be creative if we are not true to ourselves; otherwise, we will always come off as attempts at creatives, with chains on our hands and feet. To be ourselves we must have a boundless love and interest for discovering who we truly are, with all our qualities and flaws. When people talk about inner work, that's exactly what they refer to: to have a true hunger to know yourself, to get naked, to discover your deepest nature.

I wanted to study philosophy or mathematics, but in the end I chose design. I also relapsed in my doubts: After my first graduation following three years in Genoa, I went to Turin and passed the entry test for math, and I also attended a week of philosophy classes before going to Milan to continue design. I was angry for five years; I had the worst time at college, and I wished for those years to go as fast as possible. How can I unleash my true nature if I allowed that to happen? I wanted to study philosophy to follow my dream of being a writer; I wanted to study mathematics because I felt too smart to waste my talents on something "small" like design (what an arrogant prick, huh?!). In the end, I chose design because I found a good compromise between creativity and finding a job. I was scared shitless of becoming an unemployed loser. That thought kept me up at night.

One of my main concerns was wanting to succeed socially, to be recognized, even financially. I could never have dropped everything to be a writer: I would not have been able to bear the weight of that decision; I would have been crushed by it. I needed to establish myself first, to feel secure in this world, and to learn how to see myself.

I wouldn't have done half the things I did if I didn't have the courage to see why I studied design. And mind you: The positive thinking saying that goes, "There's a reason why it went that way, and in the end it was useful with Sefirot, intùiti, etc." only goes so far. It's all true, and there's more to it.

In order to awaken, we all need that *more*, the part we find most uncomfortable to look at.

Awakening no. 6

In previous exercises, is there any point where you got stuck? Where you looked at the page and thought, "I don't really know, nothing comes to mind," and you just carried on?

Okay, let's go back to that point.

Close your eyes and go back in time.

The day I told my parents that I wanted to study philosophy and not engineering, how did I feel? How did they look at me? What was my face like? What was I scared about? I can blame them and say that I compromised because of them, but is it true? At the end of the day, I was the one who decided, no one handcuffed me and drove me to the design school.

We must find the willingness to open the box that holds all of the inconvenient, explosive stuff and let it out so we can see that it wasn't that tragic after all. All right, I wanted to win at this society game; I wasn't a hippie/bohemian who didn't care about rules like my hero Henry Miller. Yep, I'm different.

In order to let go, I need some sort of financial stability. Do I suck because of that?

What did we find going back in time?

Write it down and learn to go back and really pay attention to yourself whenever something doesn't sit right. We don't need someone else to come along and ask the uncomfortable question; we can be the ones who show that kind of courage and have that kind of attention.

That's it: Let's learn to really pay attention to ourselves.

7) But it's impossible

Carlotta can't stand her job. She has been having panic attacks for five years. She even changed firms but it didn't help. When I ask her what she would really like to do, after some hesitation, and almost ashamed, she says, "Herbalist." I ask her if she knows how one can become an herbalist, but she puts her hands forward and shakes her head saying, "I'm thirty years old, who am I kidding? It's impossible."

The thought that pursuing a path is impossible is another limitation we force on ourselves. Giving up everything to be a bartender, a pizza maker, an osteopath, an artist, a juggler, an architect, a tightrope walker: heaven forbid! It always seems too late for us to change our direction. Even twenty-year-old kids say things like: "I'm afraid of throwing away three years of studies."

We often don't allow ourselves to dream because, like Carlotta, we raise our hands and stop the possibilities—we push them away. No, no, no, it's impossible. Publish a book? Me? It's impossible! To work for myself? Do you have any idea how hard it is?! To start a company? Are you nuts?!

Before opening Sefirot, I happened to show intùiti, Fabula and Cicero, the products I had already developed at the time, to entrepreneurs and consultants, and they all told me the same thing: "You'll never make money selling tools. You make money through education! Lectures, workshops, and so on." In short, they were telling me that making a living from selling tools was impossible; and to me, in all honesty, the idea of focusing on education sounded revolting: I wanted to develop products, not workshops!

Then, one morning in June 2018, I had an epiphany: I realized I knew how to sell products online (my background was in advertising and UX design), so I built a landing page (a site where interested users could "land") and set up Facebook ad campaigns for what seemed like an insane amount of money at the time: twenty dollars a day. I left the house to go climbing at the gym, thinking, "It'll never work, but fuck it, I want to try anyway." Half an hour later, when I was done with one of the circuits, I saw that one person had bought a copy of Fabula. "Just a coincidence," I convinced myself. Half an hour later, I saw another purchase. Two hours later, one more. At the end of the day I had earned one hundred twenty dollars with an investment of twenty dollars. Three days later, I decided to open the company.

Although in the following months we managed to make three hundred to four hundred dollars a day with minimal effort, when I would talk to digital marketing consultants on the phone, almost all of them would say, "It's impossible." My answer was: "Impossible my ass. Look at the data." Not even faced with numbers they would admit that this was a possible new way; they would deny the evidence. I had to review over thirty professionals and agencies before finding what became our marketing manager—the only one who replied, "Great job. I think I can do better." Beyond the impossible and even further!

Everything is impossible until we do it. And even then, there will be a lot of people who will tell us that what we're doing is still impossible, that it is working just because it is a moment, a coincidence, a trend.

Why do we act this way? Why are we so ready to tell little Leonardo da Vinci, "Flying is impossible, go build wells"?

Because the impossible is a sophisticated form of control. In ancient times they would write, "Hic abundant leones" (literally, "Lions are abundant here") to mark unexplored areas; they even thought that after a certain point the world would end. It's better to say that it is dangerous, inaccessible, and impossible, instead of finding the courage and setting off for adventure.

As Socrates used to say about the myth of the cave, where men are thought to be held captive in half-light, even if a man were to run away and discover the outside world, he wouldn't dare go back and tell the others to set them free because they would kill him instead of admitting what they think is impossible. Instead of rejoicing and saying, "Wow! So it is possible! There is something beyond that threshold!," they would rather deny the existence of something beyond it.

If we let the idea of the impossible stop us, we are allowing a line drawn by someone else fool us, a line that was made to keep us tamed. Who can be absolutely sure that you cannot become an artist at fifty? Or that you cannot leave everything behind to buy an ice-cream truck? It might be hard, risky even, but . . . impossible? Stop with the stupidity.

Awakening no. 7

What are the things that we would like to do but, deep down, think, "Please! I could never!"? Make a list:

- *To be published by a big publishing house.*
- *For a movie to be made out of one of my novels.*
- *For Sefirot to be unstoppable (to sell millions of copies to be perfectly clear).*

I know that it is possible to be published by a famous publishing house, yet deep down, I feel like it is something that I cannot reach, that it is nothing else but a dream. The same goes for the other two points. And this fear of not being destined for greatness somehow works against me.

Five years ago, I would have also written:

- *To get a positive review on* Robinson *from* La Repubblica *(it is the biggest accomplishment for an Italian writer to be reviewed in this literary insert).*
- *To have a successful company that only sells products and does no workshops and training.*

When both came true, I realized that I must have decided long before that they were plausible events. Why would I have opened an LLC if I didn't believe I could make it work? Why would I have paid a PR firm if I had not been confident that the novel was worthy of good reviews?

I had decided that it was possible, and I acted accordingly.

Let's look at what happens around us, the ambitions we deem impossible and realize that if we act as if they are impossible, by not doing anything about it, they will definitely be impossible.

Ask yourself: What would a person who is sure about the positive outcome of their endeavor do?

- *To be published by a major publishing house: send the manuscript to major publishing houses and/or find an agent.*
- *For a movie to be made from one of my novels: start writing the screenplay.*
- *For Sefirot to be unstoppable (to sell millions of copies to be perfectly clear): work on it full-time, find exceptional people to work with, network.*

If I don't go out of my way to send my manuscript, by carefully selecting the right people to talk to, like agents or publishing houses, because I think it is a waste of time, I have basically shot myself in the foot.

We have to believe that anything is possible and work toward that direction.

If we don't do it, let's think about why we want to believe that it is impossible:

- Why am I scared of being published by a major publishing house?
- Why do I prefer to wish Sefirot a limited success?

Why do we want to hold back at all costs?

8) The wish for failure

Luis and Carlo run a small company that sells eco-friendly shaving foam online. Most of the time Luis does not agree with Carlo's ideas, and vice versa; however, neither of them really stands up for their points of view—they do not talk to each other, and they waste a lot of time. Despite the fact that their company has excellent potential and acceptable profits, neither of them seems ready to put their heart and soul into it, and usually, after arguing, they both walk away saying, "It's his problem!," as if the company and its eventual failure were matters for the other person to deal with alone. They would rather complain than find a solution, and yes, your hunch is correct, as if they wanted to see the company fail.

If we were to talk to both of them individually, we would be surprised that the question: "What if the company were to close down?" would get the same answer from both: "Maybe it's better at this point" or "It would be a good excuse for me to start doing something else."

The most obvious sign that we don't actually want something is the secret hope that this something will disappear. We don't feel like going to an event, so we pray to get the call that tells us that the event has been postponed; we are fed up with our relationship and would be happy if our partner left us out of the blue; we run a business but we hope it goes bust.

We lack the courage to say no, so we wish someone else, or something else, would just close the door in our face. And usually, that's exactly what happens: A series of events unfold—like with Luis and Carlo, for instance—first their website crashes, then their ad account gets hacked, and finally, a key collaborator walks away. These might seem like misfortunes, but . . . what the heck?! None of this would have happened if they had been careful. If they really cared they would have serviced the website, paid more attention to online security, and the key collaborator would have never quit a solid team, right?

We could put it simply by saying that they are self-sabotaging in some way. They lack the courage to improve what they have and also the courage to throw in the towel and move on, so they wait for their lack of courage to bring everything down—they wait for the erosion of time.

It happened to me in relationships, when I let a love affair slide into something unbearable. I wished it would end, but I didn't have the guts to put an end to it myself. I think it has happened to many of us.

I did this at work too. The most striking episode occurred in the first months of Sefirot's life when I took a job for an outside client worth over twenty thousand dollars. I considered it only because of ego (ouch!) but I asked for a lot of money hoping that they would not accept my proposal. Instead, they said yes (darn it!), and I wanted to say no, and yet I was hoping that something would happen. I don't know what exactly—maybe that the client would collapse, or perhaps a plague of locusts would strike, that the head of product would quit and the project would be canceled, anything to get me off that job that I had no desire to do. In the end, just two days before the start, they called from London to tell me that they decided to give the job to a company they knew better. They apologized, and I thanked Jesus, the Virgin Mary, and all the archangels for that call. In retrospect, I would have been better off picking up the phone myself to say, "Sorry guys, I'm no longer available to do the job." What was the harm in that? No one was going to die.

Something similar happened years earlier, when there was a real possibility that a startup I had been working on would be incubated by the Luiss accelerator in Rome (a big private university). It would have meant moving there and working full-time on the project. Both options made me feel sick to my stomach because I had just arrived in Turin and I loved it, and the startup didn't excite me all that much. In the end, the director himself called me to tell me that, to his great regret, they ended up choosing someone else. As he explained to me in detail the reasons for the rejection, not related to the idea, but rather to risk and market factors, his voice became increasingly hesitant and confused, and I knew why: He had never heard anyone happier to have been rejected. Ha ha.

Now, in those two cases, I was okay with that. I was conscious of wanting to fail. I was looking forward to it; that's why I popped bottles and danced around the house. But if we are not aware, it can turn into a disaster. A friend of mine was given the topics to study to prepare for a public exam under the table, three sheets of possible questions. Leaving aside judgment for a system we all know is corrupt, she "lost" one of the sheets, which was the one that ended up being drawn. All her colleagues passed the test; she was the only one who failed. It is clear that she did not want that job and especially didn't want to move to another city, so she made sure to fail; still the disappointment was searing.

What will happen when Luis and Carlo fail? Because that's the direction they're heading in. Will they pop a bottle of champagne or fall into depression?

But more importantly, and this I think is the core of it all, how much time and energy do we waste doing what we don't really want to do?

How exhausted do Luis and Carlo get working on a project they don't love? How exhausted would I have been with that pointless job, or if I had gone to Rome? How much energy would I have had to use to say no in that moment? Phew, I can hardly even think about it.

The big problem is that when we commit to doing something we don't want to do with our whole self, 100 percent, we end up paying for it dearly.

Awakening no. 8

What are the aspects of our lives that we would like to improve? What about the events that we wish could be erased? We can also reference repeated episodes.

For example:

- *Last week I was asked to go to Lucca Comics (an annual comic book and game convention), and instead of planning the trip, I hoped that the city of Lucca would burn to the ground.*
- *Last year when I was asked to teach at IED (European Institute of Design), I couldn't say no, but I secretly hoped that the class wouldn't see the light of day.*

How can we avoid this from happening again?

When it comes to my habit of getting asked to do something, frowning but then entertaining the idea of doing it while I hope deep down that the offer is taken off the table, I decided to adopt a simple and efficient strategy: If the proposal makes me say, "Wow!" then I say yes; otherwise, it's a straight up no, and that's it. The energy I spend brooding over "I wonder what it would be like if I went, I wonder what would happen if, etc." is not the kind of struggle I'm willing to take on anymore

Thankfully, right now I'm not faced with a giant issue like:

- *I want the company to go bust.*

But last year something similar happened. I felt shackled by Sefirot, and I thought that maybe it would have been better to call it a day. In the end, the problem was related to my former business partner, our relationship, and the fact that I wouldn't allow myself to do anything else (I was working like a madman from morning to night), so once those issues were solved, the energy started flowing again; but the point is that if I were ever to write Sefirot in that list, I would seriously consider the idea of closing it down or changing it completely.

It is difficult but we need to find the courage to ask ourselves:

- Why do I want it to fail?
- What don't I like about the way I'm living it?
- How does it make me feel?

Even a project we love like a child can turn into a prison. This is not about betrayal. Remember how Arthur Conan Doyle tried to kill Sherlock Holmes, and Maurice Leblanc, the creator of *Arsène Lupin*, attempted the same with his character? They felt that the characters had taken over their lives, so they tried to put an end to this pain, literally killing them in the novels.

9) I want to but I don't act

Lucy works in an office but her dream is to be an actress. Will works as a copywriter in a media agency but he wants to be a writer. Peter works as a bartender but he wants to be a cook. They are different in age and lead completely different lives—Lucy is thirty-five, Will twenty-eight, Peter twenty-four—but one thing unites them: None of them are doing what they say they want to do. Lucy hasn't acted in at least two years, Will doesn't write, and Peter doesn't cook for anyone else besides himself. They talk about their big dream with everyone, but they don't walk in that direction; actually, they fill their schedules with anything that crosses their path: Lucy goes to the gym and does archery, Will picks up random freelance jobs, Peter enrolls in an acrobatic bartending class instead of a cooking class.

I have witnessed this phenomenon brought to an extreme in Los Angeles, where people flock to fulfill their dreams of greatness and then end up waiting tables. Mind you: There is nothing wrong with working a job to support yourself while trying to fulfill your ambition, except that at one point I realized that the waiters/directors, bartenders/actors, and hostesses/actresses I knew only talked about restaurants. None of them were trying to make a movie at night, or to record auditions in their spare time, or write scripts on the side.

Good-hearted people tend to justify them: "Poor people, they haven't found their place in the world yet; it must be very frustrating." True, but it doesn't help.

I wanted to be a writer, but I wasn't writing as much. I wasn't as dedicated as I was pretending to be. In short, I was a bit of a phony, a show-off who gloated in telling girls at the bar, "My dream is to be a great writer," but then, in fact, I was living the life of the art director, the publicist, the designer. Americans have a saying that goes: "Fake it until you make it," which can be a great starting point to convince yourself to be something, to give yourself momentum, but what happens if we lose ourselves in that pretense?

For the first four years of college, it looked like my real occupation was that of a writer. I went to class, I studied, I worked on projects, I did what needed to be done, and I did it with extreme efficiency and speed precisely so that I could devote myself to my novels. I was writing relentlessly five, six hours a day, in every spare moment, at the coffee shop, in bed, in the kitchen, until three in the morning, without stopping. I would go to the library to do research, walk around with my head in the clouds, thinking about the story, and its twists and turns. At that time, my "pretense" was being a designer, but the life I led was that of a writer. I wrote five novels in four years.

As I reached my senior year of college, I got scared. All my colleagues knew the names of the agencies where they would like to work, while I knew nothing and looked at the world after graduation with dread, wondering if I would be able to make it, to survive or to simply manage. The hope I was clinging onto was that something would happen, an external event, a deus ex machina that would snatch me away from the reality that was at my doorstep: I wished that a publishing house would say, "Wow, we're going to publish your book so you can focus on writing and nothing else." It didn't happen and, in a world where you work forty, fifty hours a week, my writing inspiration became harder and harder to find and use. In the following years, I had to make an effort; from time to time I would look in the mirror and force myself, "You are going to sit down and write something. Now!" It worked for a couple of months; I would write in the evening, on the weekends—I really made an effort to carve out some moments to write. At one point I even quit my job, I wrote nonstop for three months to finish a novel and then . . . then I felt lost, went back to work, and stopped writing again.

Some of you (including my past self) might argue that I was doing creative work anyway, that I was building the products with which I would launch Sefirot, that I wasn't going completely off the rails, but that's not the point.

The point is that I was saying I wanted to do something, and I wasn't doing it. One day my teacher said, "You write too little for someone who wants to be a writer." I got pissed and the only thing that calmed me down was to count the number of novels I had written when I was younger, as if those were bonuses that could guarantee me some sort of status for the years to come.

But she was right. The overwhelming and unforgiving truth is that a writer writes, an actor acts, a painter paints, a cook cooks, and a singer sings. They don't necessarily live off their passion, but they keep at it anyway. A waiter/actor who talks all day about restaurants is a waiter, not an actor. If the same person couldn't wait to get off work to go perform monologues at home in front of the camera or rehearse a show with a small, independent company, they would be leading an entirely different life.

There is no middle ground or justification for that. If we do not live the way we say we want to live, we are not even dreamers: We are just jokers. But our life becomes the joke, and it is not funny.

Awakening no. 9
Write what your dream is, if you have one.

- *To write.*

Do we talk about it with others? Do we pause every now and then, between glasses of wine, to say, "You know, what I really want to do is . . ." and with poetic flair, spill out our dream?

Now let's write next to it how many hours we dedicate to this dream each week. There is no right number. It can be one, ten, or none. Does it feel like too little, does it feel like a lot? What are the excuses that come up? But I work a lot. But I don't have much time. But I have children. But I don't sleep well. And how much time do we devote to social networks, drinks with friends, the gym, TV series, unpaid overtime instead?

No one forces us to really pursue our dreams. For now, the important thing is to be aware of reality and stop lying to ourselves. Let's look carefully at how many things we do in order not to face what we really want to do. Dare to see it. Dare to feel hurt if necessary.

And also ask yourself: Do I really want to do this?

10) To be split in two

My teacher always pointed out the phrase: "On the one hand . . . and on the other . . ." On the one hand, I would like to establish a career, and on the other hand, I don't want to give up my dreams. On the one hand, this job gives me security, and on the other hand, I crave adventure. On one side A, on the other side non-A. On one side, I like green, on the other I don't.

She was right to be so attuned to this expression because

it's often a way of beating around the bush, wasting time, and it is also very dangerous because it splits us up and over time it lengthens the distance between the two sides of ourselves that we have generated.

On one side, I like cheese, and on the other side, I don't. There is a part of me that likes it, another part that doesn't. There are two of us: One likes it and the other doesn't. The problem is that I am not two people; I am one. In the long run, I don't remember being a whole anymore; I become two (or more) who fight and don't get anything done.

Why do we split up? Because we don't want to face confrontation.

We don't like our job, so we start making a list of pros and cons. It is safe, it is close to home, it is well paid. I don't like it though, my boss is an asshole, the hours are crazy. Instead of choosing one side ("I don't like it, there's nothing more to say, better find another job" or "I need the money, I'll keep it for now"), we split. Now there is one part of us that sees the "pros" and one that sees the "cons." So we can continue to stand still and not take a stance.

The thing is that, deep down, we know that we just need to pick one side, and we usually know which one we prefer. There's an advantage in staying in the middle where you can dangle between different visions and perspectives. It's okay for a short period of time, but then, it's a no, because you end up being left dangling head down.

Awakening no. 10

What is the one thing that makes you say "On one side . . . on the other side"?

When are we whole? We don't have to solve all of our inner conflicts today; the important thing is to grasp the mechanism:

If we split, the energy is used up in the inner battle; if we become whole again we can use it to build something.

When is it that we do things halfway, holding back, not putting our entire self in it?

Let's look at something small.

Have you done the exercises you found in this book, or are you just flipping through the pages on the train, or on the bus saying, "I'll do them later"? A part of me thinks these exercises are useful, the other part is not so sure. Whether it's a small matter or a big one, it is the same story; it is a bad habit that we must get rid of. A part of me wants to write a novel, the other part doesn't. A part of me wants to work on the project, the other part doesn't. A part of me wants to succeed, the other part doesn't.

Where are we?

And on the other side . . .

And on the other side . . .

And on the other side . . .

On the other side . . .

On one side ...

Oh Lord,
how many of us
are there?

Ambush no. 1

If you're not doing the exercises, you can stop reading this book right now. It will be useless. I won't be there checking whether you're doing the work, but you will know: It's your decision.

Take responsibility for your own creative journey and do it as a whole: Either you follow it or you don't. If you choose to follow it, do the exercises; if you don't want to follow it, pick up another book.

So, which side did you choose? Ha ha.

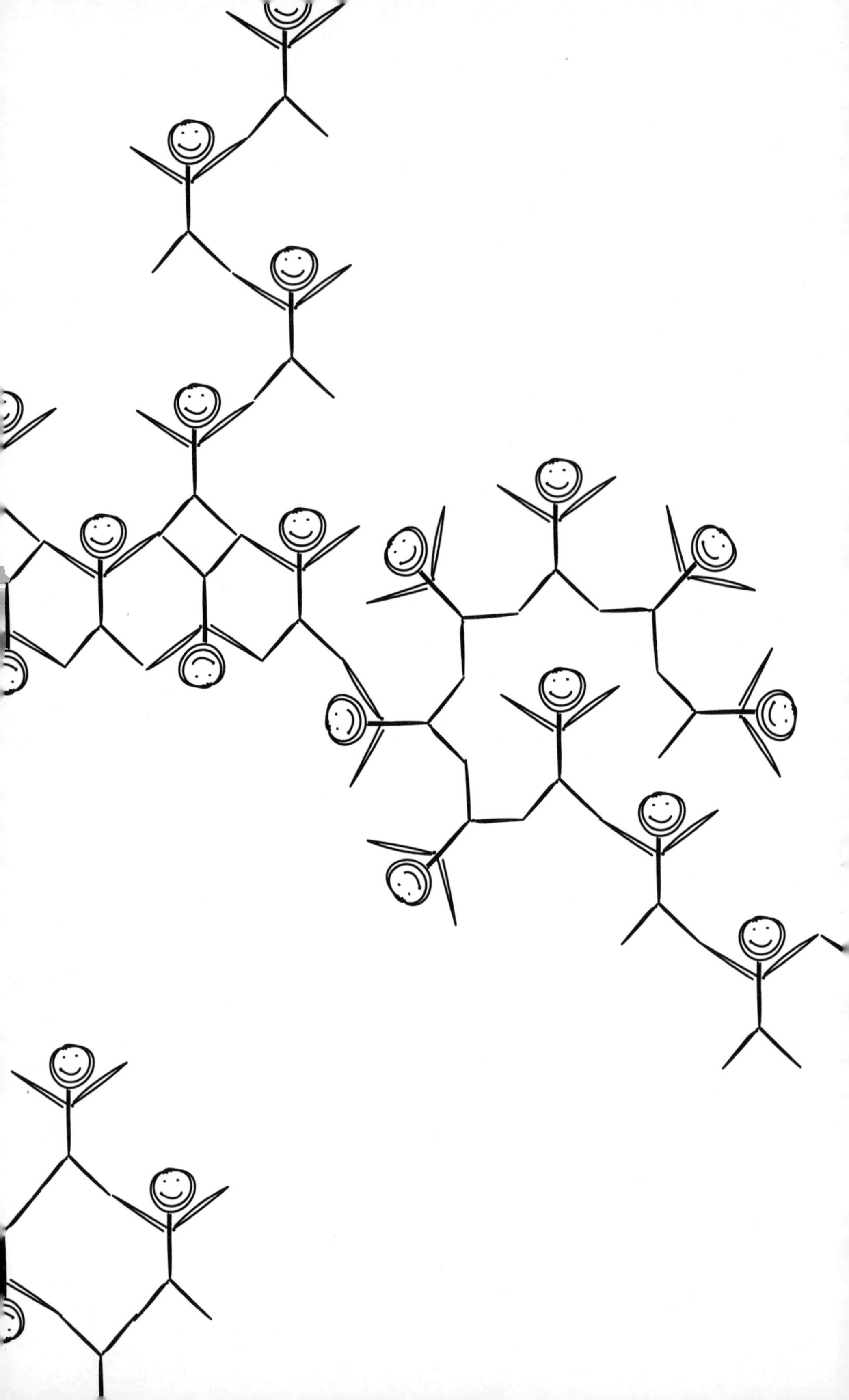

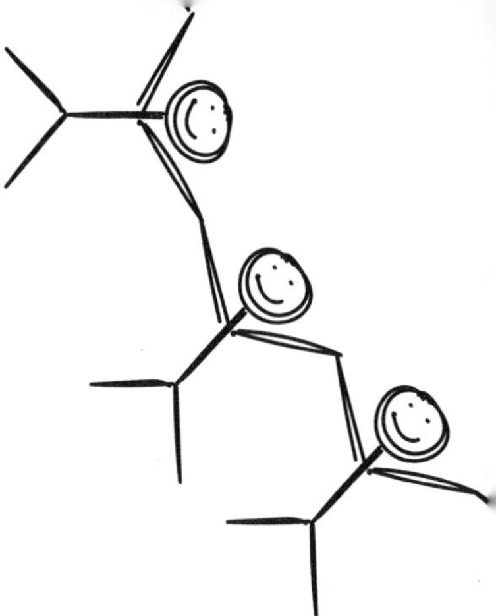

PART III

To Structure

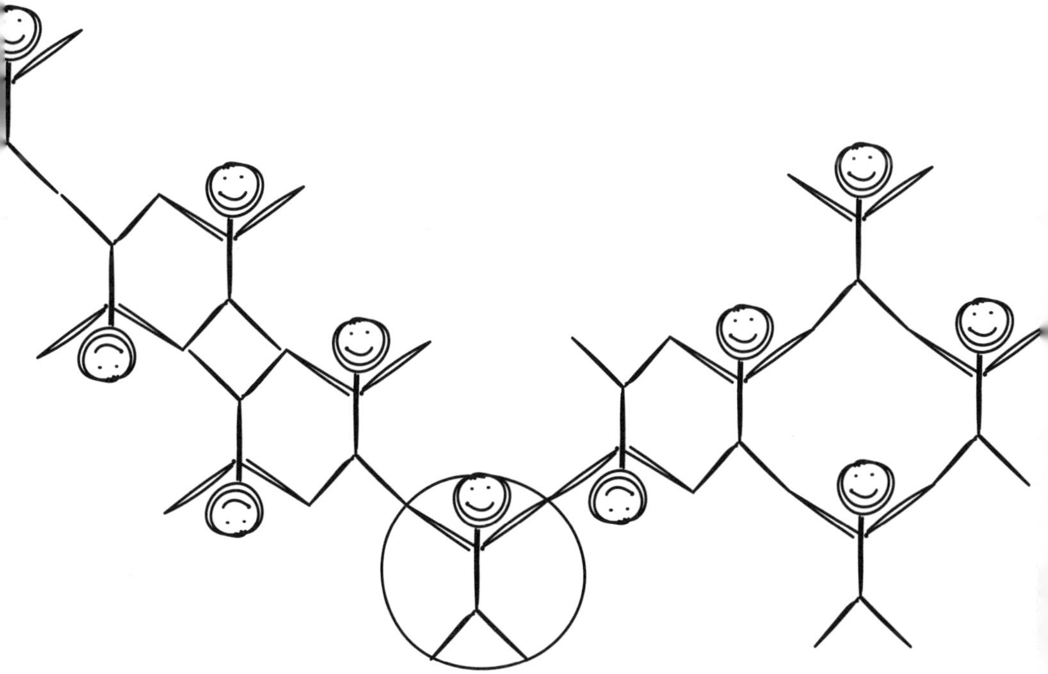

Back to the roots

When I was twenty-seven, I was in the midst of despair. I had just moved from Amsterdam to Turin to work in a big advertising agency where I was not doing well; I had started writing a new novel that seemed to be going nowhere; I had launched intùiti on Kickstarter the year before and, after an initial success, the project had stalled again. I was afraid that everything I did would lead me nowhere; I felt restless and nervous.

I went up the mountain to see my teacher and talked to her about it. And instead of pulling out the tarot cards and revealing whether I was going to publish anything, she asked me:

"Who do you want to be?"

"What do you mean?" I answered.

"Do you want to be a great writer, a great designer, or a great ad man?"

"I don't know."

"That's the problem then. You're neither here nor there."

She handed me a piece of paper and she asked me to write down the kind of life I imagined for myself: who I was, where I lived, what my days looked like, who I was with, etc.

And my mind went blank. A little bit because I thought it was stupid (I was very arrogant at the time) and a little bit because it's very hard to dream. I looked at the blank page thinking, "Why is she bugging me with this exercise? Can't she just have me pick a card so I can solve this?"

The creative path

So far we have stirred things up with the breakdowns and awakenings from the previous two sections; we tried to shake off, to poke at the frequent blockages, the limitations that were imposed by others or that we have imposed on ourselves. This is what comes most naturally to us: We have a problem, like the "blank page syndrome," or we don't know which way to go and we feel frustrated, so we look for a solution to the symptom.

We might realize that we are turned off because we are working as waiters and not in films, or because we are copywriters and not writers; we might see that we don't feel like working on a particular project because we don't have the courage to confront it, and we tend to split in two so we don't have to make a decision.

Those are all small shocks—we poke ourselves as if we were cows—and while these little things are okay to get us moving and wake us up, we are far from an actual solution.

What my teacher tried to explain to me when she asked, "Who do you want to be?" is that it is not possible to face the superficial symptom with a snap of your fingers. I feel like I haven't found my way, I get an epiphany, and bam, the issue is solved. That desperation, the feeling like an eel in a barrel, is a warning: "Hey, take a closer look." It is a way to bring back the attention toward yourself, to understand that the wheels are not turning, something is blocking and limiting me causing me to suffer. It is useful for realizing that the real problem lies deeper, and it is a structural one—it's about how I set up my creative life.

What we are going to do from now on is start from the basics, go to the roots and trace a new trail to follow, nurture and expand our creativity.

The fundamental matter: Who am I?

Let's grab a piece of paper, or a notebook, and write down these questions:

- Who am I?
- What do I want? (focus on practical matter).
- What impact do I have on the world?

Let's define ourselves and start imagining our life.
For example:

- *I am a writer.*
- *I am famous, I sold millions of copies.*
- *My books make children dream.*

Let's write all sentences in the present tense, as if we've already achieved what we desire. And let's write without fear or shame; in fact, let's challenge ourselves to dare and dream the unthinkable.

- *I am an entrepreneur.*
- *I have ten million dollars in my bank account.*
- *My products help tens of thousands of people.*

It could be anything:

- *I am the greatest creative in the world.*
- *Everyone calls me for consultations.*
- *I help people better express themselves.*

Or even:

- *I am a chef.*
- *I own a restaurant.*
- *Anyone who eats at my place is happy.*

We need these questions to explore who we would like to be on a practical level, to stimulate our imagination and visualize the way we would like to live.

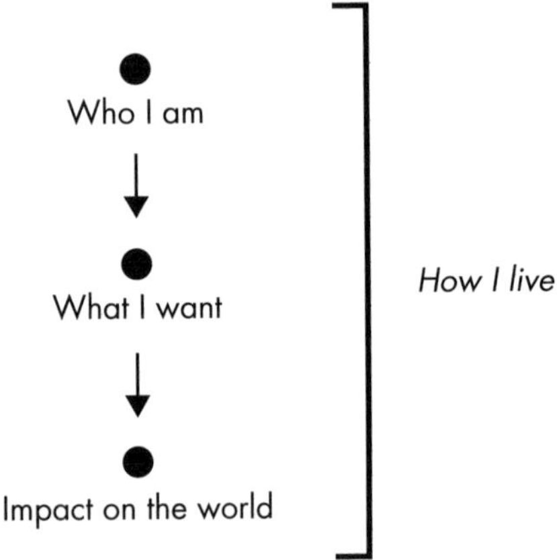

It is a genuine exercise on imagination and visualization. Let's try to get into the details. What does our day look like? What time do we wake up? Where do we live? Who do we live with? What do we eat?

I live in Turin in a big house with a terrace. I wake up in the morning and write from 8 a.m. to noon. Afterward, I go out and eat at a restaurant near my house. In the afternoon, I read books, meet other writers, and sometimes I teach in a school. In the evening, my partner comes home and we have dinner together.

Do I enjoy it? Does it bore me? And what don't I like? Is there something I would like to change?

I live in Lisbon in a big house with a terrace. I wake up in the morning and write from 8 a.m. to noon. Afterward, I go out and eat at a restaurant near my house. In the afternoon, I read books in a café, play sports, and walk around the city. Occasionally, I teach creative writing online. In the evening, my partner comes home and we go out. We have many friends.

Better? Is there anything still missing? Am I satisfied or not? Let's try with another example:

I live in Turin in a large house with a terrace. I run my business remotely, and I am a successful entrepreneur. I wake up early and coordinate with my team. I am often on the phone, telling others what to do. At lunch, I go out to eat at a restaurant near my home. In the afternoon, I start working again; I have a very busy life. People call me for consultations, and I try to manage everything. In the evening, my partner comes back home and we have dinner together.

Do I like this? Honestly, I feel a bit lonely and all that being on the phone doesn't sound too cool. I'll try again.

I live in Turin in a big house with a terrace. I wake up, have breakfast, read for half an hour, and then go to the office. It's downtown, and I can walk there. In the office, I work with my team: We are like a family—I like them a lot—and we have both a good work and personal relationship. We tackle each day like it is an adventure. At lunch, we eat together. I have a busy life that I really enjoy. Sometimes we work late, and I feel we are all passionate about what we do. Often my partner picks me up from the office, and we have a glass of wine around there.

All right, this works better but I might add:

I spend very little time on the phone. I have a personal assistant who filters out the less important phone calls and helps me stay focused, easing my workload.

As I mentioned above, the first time I was asked to do this exercise, I thought it was a waste of time, pure nonsense, but guess who the sucker was?

If you find it difficult to do it, don't get frustrated, it's normal. That's just the way it is: It is not only difficult but very difficult. Being able to synthesize who you want to be is exhausting, either because we do not yet know who we want to be, or because we do not have the courage to admit it. My advice is to try, to write by hand on your sheet, and then erase and rewrite until a sentence or an image comes out that resonates with you and makes you say, "Okay! I like that!"

Start doing it as if it were a game, and fill the page according to how you feel today, knowing that nothing is definite, tomorrow we might want to be someone else, and that's okay.

I've had times in my life when I've said, "I'm an ad man," and other times when I felt like saying, "I'm a writer," "a multidisciplinary creative," "a great UX designer," "a businessman," and in fact, I've been all those things.

The power of this exercise is that we are charting the way to materialize who we are and what we want.

Responsibility and reality

What happens when we start standing up for who we say we want to be? I want to be a writer, and I start writing every morning. I want to be published, and I start contacting all the publishing houses and literary agents that I am interested in. I want to be a cook, and I enroll in a class. I actually employ energy to express the person I feel I am.

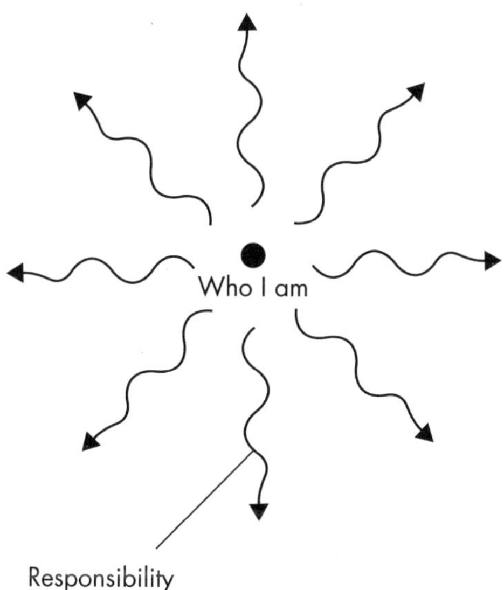

This entails *responsibility*. I have to decide that I want to support who I am. I have to commit myself. I cannot just dream of a different life and then do something else entirely. That's when something happens—the energy I put out and my actions produce an effect.

I believe that the universe gives us back who we are and especially who we feel we are. So if I am a writer and feel like a writer, the universe will give me a writer's life. We can apply the same concept to other belief systems, spiritual or not: If we ask to be writers, God will make sure to help us (Jesus said, "Ask and you shall receive") or, in a more secular view, if we start living like writers, we will indeed have a writer's life.

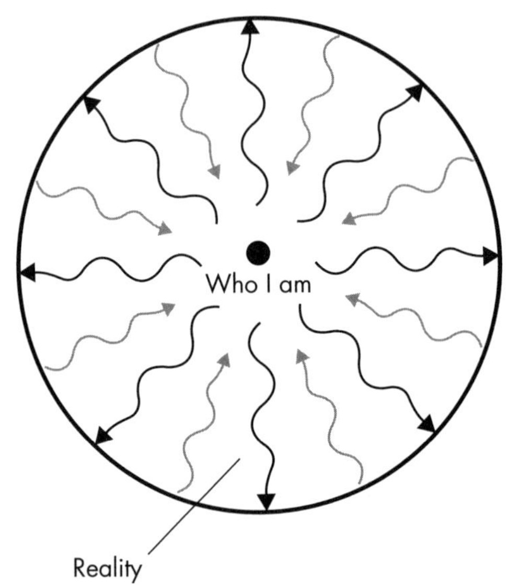

This "return" of energy and response plunges us into a new world, a new *reality*, which is a direct consequence of who we decide to be.

When I opened Sefirot, I decided that I was going to be an entrepreneur, more specifically a publisher: The day after going to the notary, my partner and I took a trip to Poland to learn about a company that specialized in printing cards. At the airport I met a girl who asked me, "What do you do?" I did not answer, as I would have done the week before, "I am a multidisciplinary creative." Instead I said, "I'm a publisher." "Wow," she said, "and what do you publish?" I showed her our website, and she bought a copy of intùiti right in front of me.

I was who I wanted to be, and the universe provided me with a sale. Or, I was who I wanted to be, and as a result, I told a girl about Sefirot and she bought intùiti. Action and reaction. If I had told her, "I am a writer," we would have talked about one of my books.

We have the incredible power to be able to contribute to the creation of our reality. That is, as long as we take responsibility: if we write that we are one thing, then we have to stand for it, to be it. If we write that we are writers, then we have to write. If we write that we are publishers, then we have to open the company and go to Poland to see how to print cards. If we write that we want to be the greatest advertisers in the world, then we have to spend time on LinkedIn to find a job in New York, London, Paris; it doesn't work if we stay stuck in the ad agency in a small town in the middle of nowhere. If we write that we want ten million dollars in our bank account, we have to commit to making our company grow.

And the most important aspect is the kind of reality that is given back to us, which gives us the opportunity to experience what we say we want to be.

In 2015, while I was between jobs, I lived as a writer for three months, and I realized that there was something I didn't like too much about that reality: to write, to dream at night about my characters like they were an obsession, and then to finish the book and think, "Okay, now what?" I realized I wanted to be a more versatile figure.

From 2018 to 2021, I was an entrepreneur. I worked a ton, achieved a lot, and also saw that I was shutting down and heading into burnout. I reimagined my life to make sure that I could write every day. It's been a year and a half now since

I started writing in the mornings and doing business in the afternoons.

To sum it up: Our responsibility is to support who we want to be so that we can experience the reality we say we want.

If we say we are writers, we must live like the kind of writer we have envisioned. If we say we are chefs, we must live like a chef, and that applies to everything and everyone. And, if we don't like it, we must have the courage to revise what we thought we wanted.

In addition, the three points we saw earlier—who I am, what I want, and what impact I make—must be aligned and consistent, otherwise that reality doesn't hold up. If I want to be a big, rich advertiser, I have to move in a direction that will allow me to make a lot of money. If I want to be a surfer who doesn't work but I want to be rich and able to support my family, maybe there is something misaligned in my vision, unless I was born rich or won the lottery. This exercise helps us move within a plausible reality, not the limited reality of those who say, "That's impossible," but the reality we can be responsible for, the reality we want to help build.

**Frequently asked question: "But I don't know what I want!"*

Here we go back to one of the things we saw in the first sections. If we don't know what we want and we persist in pretending, the exercise doesn't work because it would be like saying, "I am everything and nothing," and the result is what happened to me when I was twenty-seven years old: doing everything and nothing, getting everything and nothing, and feeling restless and without a clear path to follow.

In this case, it is best to choose a temporary path (which is always better than standing at the crossroad like fools); for example, we could say, "I'm a writer," and try to go down that path for a time, to live the experience. Or admit that we don't yet know what we want to be and turn that into an advantage: "I am open." We can choose to be flexible, to let dozens of paths sweep us for a time, so that we open twenty different doors and then choose the one that we want to walk into.

An example

Sonia says she wants to be a game designer; however, when she has a chance to enroll in a course on the subject, she decides not to; she says she wants to take it easy this year—she is not in a hurry—so for a few months she would like to live as a digital nomad.

Sonia is free to do what she wants, and depending on how she goes about it, her life will take different turns. The only problem arises if there is a lack of accountability: If she says, "I'm a game designer," while declining to enroll in the game design course to be a digital nomad, then she needs to review her statement and change it to "I am a digital nomad," and at that point she goes on living as a digital nomad.

In a nutshell, if Sonia does not enroll in the course this year and she decides to leave town to be a digital nomad, who is Sonia? A somewhat lost, irresponsible person who says something but doesn't do it, and she will have exactly that kind of life until she realigns.

Ambush no. 2

If accountability is missing, everything is missing. If you say you want to do something and you don't do it, you are not responsible; you are not able to back up your words. So you start living a random reality, lost in a numbness that can last for years and leave you exhausted; be careful. At that point creativity can't help you, and there are no exercises or techniques that can make you feel alive and fulfilled. No framework, no lateral thinking, no class, not even a mentor can help you. Because you have not mapped out the path: You might have complained about it, maybe played it cool while mentioning it, but it is not the same thing as doing it.

How creativity works

In February 2011, I was having a beer outside a club in the neighborhood of Bovisa, in Milan. I was twenty-three years old, I don't remember who I was with. I was probably with some of my college friends, or some other friends who had tagged along. I don't even remember what we were talking about. About our courses, I guess, about the school, about what we were enjoying and what we weren't. I must have complained about the lack of creativity that I felt everywhere at the Milan Polytechnic, the school I was attending. I had a gut feeling that was making me nervous; it seemed that the thing I was looking for—creativity—was just not there, period. And this awareness was cutting into me like a razor blade stuck in my stomach.

Then I remember looking toward the long street that ended in Bausan Square. A car stopped at the traffic light; its headlights were so bright they blinded me. I remember standing there deliberately staring without squinting at the two yellow lights widened by the fog. It was a very brief moment—the car started, turned right, and disappeared—but I had seen something in the glare.

I turned to one of my friends and said, "I would like to make cards. Cards for creativity."

Who I am today and what I do is derived from that insight. How did it land on me? Who sent it to me? No one knows. Is it a trick of the brain or a handout from above? Who knows. Does it make any difference to us to know? Would I have been able to sit at a small table and make an effort to come up with such an idea? I don't think so.

The next day, I did not start working on what would become intùiti, which saw the light of day two years after that night. Not even the following week. I don't know how long I let that intuition ripen. I do remember, though, that during a class, when the professor came up to us and said, "The work in my class is to design what you feel like," I stood up and said, "I'd like to build a deck of cards for creativity."

He said, "Go talk to my ex–business partner," and at that moment, he mentioned the woman who would become my teacher.

Feminine and masculine

What I described in the anecdote has happened to me many other times: a hunch comes, unexpectedly, and then, perhaps, an action follows, a push to put it into practice.

Seeing the cards is the intuition; deciding to work on them is the action. The first is not within our control, it just comes to us; the second, on the other hand, is up to us; we are the ones who choose to pursue an idea or not.

These two "phases" represent our feminine and masculine principles: The feminine welcomes, feels, dreams, while the masculine puts into practice, strives with discipline and rigor.

This is not to be confused with divergent and convergent thinking, because divergent thinking, as we will see later, is incited by something specific; whereas, when we speak

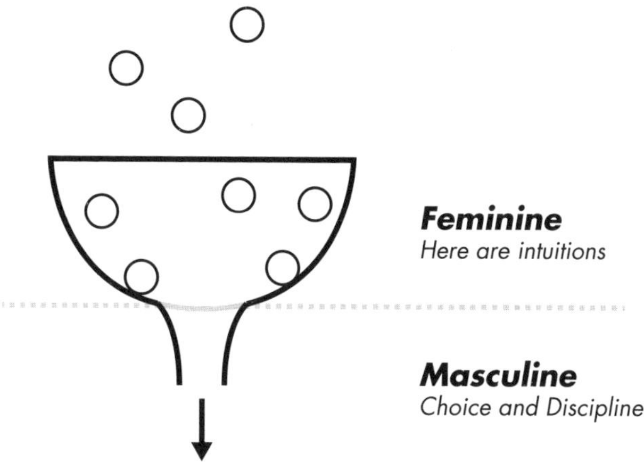

of the feminine, we mean a natural impulse, a free-flowing inspiration.

As you can see in the illustration, our feminine part receives from above and is filled with ideas, insights, images. When we are in the shower and we get a flash of genius, that is our feminine part working. When we have a dream, it is always the feminine part, the unconscious that lights up. Our feminine part is the lightest (in the sense of non-heavy), the funniest, the most open and welcoming, the most spontaneous.

If we operated only with the feminine part, we would be like an overflowing cup, which, however, never succeeds in putting anything into practice. We need the masculine principle as well; when we choose one of our intuitions and say, "Yes, this is good, I'm going to pursue it," "Yes, I want to write this story," "Yes, I have decided to go abroad," or "Yes, I want to open that company," that is our masculine side talking. When we force ourselves to wake up every morning at seven o'clock to write, when we don't go out in the evening because we have a deadline, that is the masculine. Our masculine side is the most decisive, the most responsible (and sometimes burdensome), the coldest and the most calculating; it is the disciplined and stubborn one, the one that slams its fist on the table.

We need both:

- **If we only operate within our feminine side.** We become like Gregory whose example we saw in the early chapters: an endless stream of ideas that never come to fruition, excessive and almost compulsive, unable to keep his feet on the ground and who gets carried away by intuitions like a balloon in the breeze. He lacks the practicality and discipline to choose one of the many ideas and pursue it.
- **If we only operate within our masculine side.** We become incapable of dreaming; we only stick to numbers and logic. We are no longer capable of having an original idea, and in the worst cases, we even try to bend the feminine to our will.

Be careful of the masculine bending the feminine. This is what happens in most creativity techniques out there, mostly in brainstorming and related divergent thinking: Our masculine side gets pissed off because he cannot control the feminine, so he locks her in a room and forces her to birth ideas. When we are in environments where we have to come up with ideas and there is a struggle, the struggle is the masculine trying to dominate the feminine. Those who have worked in advertising agencies know what the feeling is: When we have come up with a couple of decent ideas, we are not satisfied, but just relieved; because we've done it, we can go home and relax.

**Frequently asked question: "What if I have to come up with ideas for work, what do I do? Do I refuse to?"*

That's a great question. Think about your feminine and masculine as two separate people, standing one in front of the other, who must live together, work together, and help each other out. The first one is a determined man. He knows what to do and stomps his feet—stomp, stomp, stomp—he's ready for action. The other one is a free woman, so powerful that no one can force her into anything; her beauty lies in staying up watching the moon till late at night. I think of my masculine and feminine as an army general and a witch, but you can picture them however you like.

For example, if I get a request from a creative director who says, "Matteo, can you come up with a couple of ideas for this campaign?," the general stands at attention while the witch couldn't care less. The general says, "Woman, we must work!" while she looks at him and then laughs in his face. We often look at the feminine as the nurturing, motherly side, but that's wrong; the feminine is mostly an untamable force, impossible to contain, proud and destructive when she's angry.

The general can grab the witch by her hair and put her to work, but we have already seen that it's not nice and it doesn't work so well, or else he can respect her. And respecting her means recognizing her freedom, and yes, even her being temperamental and irrational. The witch, on her part, will take advantage of the general's willpower and strategic and logical skills to achieve goals.

To answer the question: We must learn to respect our feminine side, to nurture it and play along with it. It's an internal attitude, like sitting down in front of the page saying, "Okay, let's see what comes up," instead of "Now you have to sit and write something down, for crying out loud." People who adopt the first approach are those who, at some point, follow the feminine side altogether and quit their jobs if they do not like what they are doing; those who adopt the second, on the other hand, usually end up working in the same place for years even if they feel miserable.

Train the feminine side

During brainstorming sessions in the agency, I used to have a lot of fun. I would enter a dimension where I didn't so much care about coming up with an idea as I cared about having fun in the research, in the possibilities, even if it was nonsense, even if I opened my mouth and bullshit would come out; it happened often that immediately after saying something I would laugh. Until the moment when I was no longer enjoying myself: It could happen after an hour, or after five; if I began to feel that something was closing in, that the room was becoming gray, that the faces around me looked discouraged, then I no longer felt like going on, and it felt it would have been better to resume later on or another day.

Not everyone felt the same way; they looked at me like I was volatile when I would stand up and say, "All right, shall we continue tomorrow?" or "Should we continue at the bar? Anyone feel like drinking coffee? Maybe a spritz?" Those who stayed in the room staring at each other usually accomplished very little, besides getting a headache. I would get ideas on my way to the bar, or if nothing came up, I would start feeling better and return to a state where ideas could come more easily.

To train your feminine side means to learn how to be open. You cannot train the feminine side, because it already knows everything. What we can do is to train ourselves to be more open and receptive, to honor our irrational part, to follow and go along with it. We need to become more sensitive (in the sense of "feeling more") and try to enlarge the cup in the image above so that it allows us to collect as many marbles as possible.

It means listening to one's instincts, hunches, dreams, and having the courage to trust them.

On my first day at the agency in Turin, I went to talk to the HR manager. I had moved back from Amsterdam in a rush because they needed me to start immediately. The woman sitting across the table explained to me how my contract worked when it came to time off and sick leave. Then she gave me the card to clock in and out. "Before nine thirty in the morning," she said, "and starting from six in the evening." She also added, "But usually people leave later than that." I asked her if it was necessary to clock out so they could calculate overtime, but she said that according to company policy, overtime was not paid. On seeing my face twitch, she smiled and said, "We know that in your line of work you often overwork, and for that reason, we gift you an extra hour per month for doctor's appointments!"

At that exact moment, a voice in my head said, "Matteo, leave. Leave now. You will not be happy here. You will be miserable." It wasn't so much for the unpaid overtime (ad agencies apply that policy often, but that wasn't what upset me); it was more of a bigger feeling: the HR woman smiling at me like a weasel, the crappy white office inside a fascist building, the faces of those I had seen walking by that didn't seem too thrilled.

That was my feminine. It already knew it was going to be shitty, that I was going to get vertigo from stress, that I was going to learn something, sure, that I was going to embellish my résumé a bit with a big name, but . . . was it really worth it? At the end of life, we don't get a medal for being miserable.

On June 3, 2014, I did not follow my feminine because my masculine took over. "You already signed the contract," it said, "you left Amsterdam after two years. You rented an apartment. This was an investment. It is so prestigious to work here. What are you? A child?" I imagine that our masculine all sound the same. It wasn't wrong—it made sense—but that's exactly the point: The feminine doesn't stop to think, the feminine feels. The contract could have been canceled in a heartbeat, the apartment was cheap (four hundred fifty dollars per month). It would have not been a problem, but I couldn't do it.

It is very difficult to follow the feminine because we have to jump without a safety net, without any supporting rational argument. If we want to blow a deal, it is easier to do it because "the math doesn't add up" and not "because my gut told me to." We are not used to following our instincts and, understandably so, we are terrified of them.

In June 2018, four years after I started working at the agency, I was faced with a similar situation once more. A former classmate of mine had suggested starting a company with him and his father, who had been a big shot at a global consulting firm. The plan was simple: We would build a team and daddy would open the rolodex for us filled with relationships he had acquired during his career. Projects were going to pour in nonstop, along with revenues. I had even involved two of my friends in this operation, but at the time of the final arrangements, when all five of us (my former classmate, his father, my two friends, and me), were sitting around the same table, I hesitated.

The little voice showed up again: "No, Matteo, don't do it. Something is wrong here." My masculine answered, "What are you talking about? These are good people. Solid people. The deal is good. And you got two of your friends on board. You can't throw everything away because of a hunch. You're going to look bad!"

Fortunately, I had changed over those four years: This time I decided to be irrational, uncontainable. I looked at them and said that I had some doubts, that I wasn't sure anymore. That sentence was enough for everything to crumble. My ex-colleague's father became stiff and told me with the most disgusting, condescending paternalism in his voice: "Matteo, you can't always be a lone wolf." I felt like flipping the table over and throwing a chair at his head, but I kept calm. I just chuckled and replied, "Okay, whatever you say." I proceeded to tell him that I was out, and it was the best decision I have ever made: Two months later I opened Sefirot.

Do you see it? Opening up to ideas and intuitions is not only a matter of sitting down in front of a piece of paper and saying, "C'mon, send an idea." It is a much more disruptive process that requires solid faith in our irrational side, the one we can't explain.

Why did I get the idea for intùiti? I get asked that a lot during interviews. I answer that I didn't feel a lot of creativity when I attended the Milan Polytechnic and yada yada, but the truth is: I don't know. Why did I get the idea for Fabula? For Sefirot? For my novels? I have no clue. Of course I could try to piece together a meaning, to find reasons that will stand and be interesting when I tell them during a TEDx, but deep down, I know that the reason is beyond my grasp.

This is the great madness-courage combo that comes by following the feminine: I worked for two years on an idea that came to me without me knowing why it arrived; and I worked five years more to find a way to divulge it. And this is exactly what creatives do, in every field, constantly: They strive to turn into reality something they have sensed, without knowing why they felt it. We all want to find a justification for this behavior because otherwise it would mean that we are delusional or, worse, incompetent. Then again, who would invest all this energy for something they only "felt"? Ha ha. The core of the whole issue about the feminine lies right here: I don't know it, but I feel it. And feeling is everything. I feel I want to do it. I feel I'm going in that direction. I feel that today it is more right for me to eat fish and not meat, to take a different route, to go home earlier, to go for a run, to write, or to sleep. There is no rational motivation. The only motivation is that I feel I want to do exactly that.

Accepting this part of us and respecting it is the first real step toward our creativity.

Training system to open up to the feminine

I don't know for certain if there's a universal formula for everyone to learn to trust their feminine side more. What I can do is share what has worked for me, drawing from my experience with my teacher, Alessandra Mazzucchelli, whom I had the opportunity to follow in several seminars on Interpersonal Communication that she led.

1) Work on the body

What limits our capability of feeling is the mind. We think, and we think a lot. Not only that, we are often taught that rational, logical thinking is a plus, a superpower. I used to brag about being able to think sharply, surgically, precisely, to be able to win an argument by turning tables better than others, and to always manage to be right, even at the cost of making the other person exasperated using proof by contradiction. My teacher used to get angry when I did that to her. She would say, "Okay, good for you, you are right. And what now? You are boring. So, so boring!" I would get sad and not understand. And that was the catch: I wanted to understand, to categorize, put inside a box, and I refused to feel. This is an attitude very much associated with the masculine: One plus one is two, and there's no way it could be different. For the feminine, one plus one is eleven. And that's what opens you up to another realm.

The most frequent problem I encounter when doing intùiti sessions is the very same resistance I used to put up with my teacher: rational thinking. The most stuck people are the ones who want to understand, who strive to reason, to find a solution to their lack of drive, of passion, of openness, and they want to do it with their minds. I try to explain that they can't get there following a string of thoughts: They have to move to another level; they have to open their hearts and breathe, and they look at me like I'm uttering fortune cookie–type sentences. So I ask them to close their eyes and take a few deep, belly breaths. Usually four or five are enough; and that's usually when they put their hands on the table and say, "No, no, that's enough." They felt something and they got scared.

My teacher told me for years, "You can only get to a certain point using your head. Then, you have to get your body involved." And I couldn't understand (here we go again) what the heck she was talking about. What about the body? How was that going to change anything? Then one day, she made me do an exercise using a bioenergetic technique, a psychotherapeutic method that uses breathing exercises and body vibration: She asked me to stand with my knees slightly bent, eyes closed, and to breathe from the belly. I was stuck, a toy soldier made of lead, so much that on the third breath I started to feel dizzy and had to run into the pathway and walk back and forth to get back on my feet. The mind was short-circuited, the world upside down. What on earth had happened?

1 + 1 = 11 (wow)

I then went to a bioenergetic analyst for years, and I was reeducated in the art of feeling.

I would flood her with words, very well-constructed thoughts, and she would stop me and ask, "Where do you feel it in your body?" And every time she said that, I felt like I lost my balance. What do you mean, in the body? It took me months and months to realize that besides thoughts, I was full of feelings. Belly ache, discomfort in my hands, warmth in my throat.

Sometimes I felt comfortable and other times I did not, and that the ease and discomfort came earlier and sharper than the thoughts I later created to find an explanation for the feeling. One day in the subway in Milan, a guy came up behind me as I was getting a ticket at the machines. He reached out to select the ticket for me, and then looked at me expecting to get some spare change. I didn't have time to think about how to act; I turned to him and shouted, "Why did you do that?!" Then I felt ashamed of that spontaneous reaction and I ran away.

We feel so many things—I like it, I don't like it, I'm fine, I'm not fine, I'm hot, I'm cold, I'm comfortable, I'm angry, I'm upset, I'm bored, etc.—and often, instead of trusting our feelings and letting them guide us, we think about the reason why we felt that way and try to control the flow.

The problem is that intuition is part of that feeling, and it is very difficult to let ideas flow if we are filtering them with thoughts.

I have always had ideas, or even true epiphanies, anytime I pushed my body to exhaustion. Going for a run, even when I was younger, there was a moment when I felt as if something was released within me, and my body would go on its own and my mind would be forced to vanish for a few moments, and then enlightening connections would come to me. It could have been scenes from a book I was writing, or resolutions for a project, or other considerations that I had under my nose all along but never noticed. One day, I remember realizing that I was in love with a girl and doing everything I could not to feel it. That realization hit me like a slap in the face. I stopped in my tracks, I looked at the plowed field in front of me, and I said aloud, "Shut up! Really?!"

We don't want to feel, because it can be very uncomfortable, and thinking helps us block the feeling, and the thoughts crystalize in our bodies, making us more rigid. If we can distract the body, to break it a little bit, to relax the muscles, to let it vibrate, that's when the capability of feeling comes again!

To this day, when I go for a run along the river Dora in Turin, there is a tree-lined avenue exactly halfway down my route, and I know that when I run there, ideas come flowing to me. I don't look for them; they just come. Sometimes it's a good idea, something that helps me for a novel, or for a project; other times it's awful shit. My only commitment is to get there and be open.

Exercise no. 1A

Start trusting your body. Engage in small experiments. Go out for a walk either to go to work or to get to an appointment, and let your body guide you. Try to listen to it: Today, do my feet want to go left or right? Do my feet want to walk on this side of the street or on the other? Don't ask questions, just try to go along. The head turns to look at a window, and we feel tempted to stop even if we don't understand why: That's okay, stop. Do we get a hunch to go back and change route? Try it, do it. Yes, even if you feel dumb knowing that people are looking at you as you zigzag through the streets. So what? Look at it as a game and play along.

Then slowly, start doing it more often, even when you're at home. Does your hand move toward the white mug instead of the red one? Go along. Do we pick up the lighter pair of jeans instead of the ones we thought we would wear? Trust your hand! Here lies the whole point: Start trusting that thing that is guiding you even if you cannot explain it, whether it is instincts, intuition, or whatever you want to call it. Try to listen to it until you are able to feel it more clearly. Then, one evening at a dinner party, you will feel like getting up and leaving, or when faced with a contract to sign, you will be unable to pick up the pen in front of you. And you will find that it was the best thing for you, and you already knew it.

It will happen that we were planning to go out with a friend, but instead we will feel the urge to sit at our desk and that will be the day when we will write the first chapter of our book.

We will discover that there is something inside us that knows better than we do what needs to be done.

Exercise no. 1B

Try to bring your body into vibration or exhaustion. Go for a run, take a walk, dance, exercise, try to get to the point where the body is forced to take over, to tell us, "I know what I have to do: I must put one foot in front of the other, and you cannot control anything anymore."

We can do this with dynamic meditations like Osho's, whose explanations and music you can find online, or by practicing deep, belly breathing (it would be best to do this the first few times with someone who can support and help you).

We can also do this by listening to cumbia or another type of music we like and dance until we break a sweat. Or we can spin on ourselves, as we did as children, get dizzy and fall to the floor while the world spins some more.

We can even fall asleep on the couch with an iron wrench in our hand, or another object that can fall to the floor, the noise of which will wake us up as soon as we get into a state of deep sleep.

In short, let's find a way to mess us up, to make ourselves less stiff, let's become softer, freer, and see if something happens.

2) Meditate

Let me start by saying that I don't like meditating. I never liked it that much, and my teacher told me to do it for years,

until one day when she said, "If you don't start meditating, we might as well call it a day," I groaned, gave in, and started doing it. In the end, as usual, she was right. Ha ha. She taught me to meditate in the simplest way possible: Sit in a chair with your back straight, eyes closed, hands on your legs, palms upward, mouth slightly ajar trying to curl a smile.

What have I learned by meditating? That there are a lot of thoughts going through our heads: "Ah, this sucks," "I'm meditating," "Oh man, how much longer?," "Oh okay, I'm getting good at this, I managed to do it for a bit." Then, after those first thoughts, we start thinking about what needs to be done the next day, and the day after that, then we start going off on a tangent, and we think about an old love story, our current relationship, a sex scene, a Christmas present, a worry, the pain we feel in our back, a dreadful itch in our leg, and so on.

All those thoughts are the main problem. The mind holds us in its web of thoughts, and often those thoughts are not even our own; they are hearsay, phrases that someone else is thinking that we somehow perceive, and they slip into our stream, like when we quickly scroll through Instagram or Facebook, and those "posts" crowd our minds.

Meditating can help us witness this disaster and choose which thoughts to hold on to and which need to go. I think about my cat playing, I like it, I keep it. I think about what I have to do tomorrow, and it generates anxiety, partly because I can't do anything about it until I sit down and do it. Then I let it go, swoosh, gone. Little by little we can manage not to think about anything, to get to what is called the non-mind, a state where we are empty, because we have gotten rid of the pile of uselessness. We empty the cup, and at that point, insight can come and fill it up.

Exercise no. 2

We do not have to become great meditators, practicing for hours a day (that is not the purpose of this book—if you want to take that route, there are much more suitable texts). We can start with about ten minutes each morning and then increase little by little, if we like the practice. We can do it sitting in a chair, with a straight back, or on the floor in the lotus position, or even lying on the bed, as long as we don't fall asleep. We can also do it walking down the street, moving slowly and looking at the ground fifty inches beyond our feet.

What matters is that we focus on the thoughts that come, give them a name ("work," "concern about the house," "financial fear," "hypochondria"), and if we don't care to delve into them, let them go. More will come, and then some more, and one by one, try to let them go. There will be thoughts that we fall into, that will make us forget that we are meditating, that will carry us far away. No problem: When we notice, we go back and let it go.

The goal is to start asking for something, an insight or an idea. Let's really try to ask for it: "Give me something." We can imagine it coming from above or from within. Let's start feeling like antennae that are able to pick up something more than the hubbub in our heads. Maybe a silly thing comes along, to add sun-dried tomatoes and almonds (almonds, really?) to the spinach we were going to cook for lunch; maybe we get the title of the book we are writing.

We begin to form a relationship with this inexplicable, mysterious, somewhat mystical, and even somewhat magical feminine.

3) Dreams

The feminine includes the realm of the unconscious, the netherworld that opens up the moment we close our eyes and

our brain enters a different state, during which we lose control. The dream is the perfect example of the experience of the feminine: We are guided and, more often than not, pulled into an unexpected and surprising journey that we cannot escape from and that has a major impact on us when we wake up. Who hasn't woken up suddenly after a nightmare? Or has been troubled by an image from a dream and then rushed to find its meaning in an attempt to gain some relief?

Or even to be cheerful and invigorated throughout the day just because of a wonderful dream? Or to be inspired by it? Thousands of works of art have sprung up this way.

And talking about dreams, there is no scientific or rational explanation. What happens to our brain while it produces nighttime images has been studied, and still there is no explanation for why we dream and what it might really mean. Some say it is a mechanism for cleansing our emotions; others speculate that it may be an evolutionary system, whereby we test ourselves with new situations to find out what effect they have on us.

I honestly don't care too much about that. What I find most fascinating is the transition from our daytime self to our nighttime self: We close our eyes, surrender to sleep, and finally no longer have control over our thoughts and the images we generate; someone else comes along, a deep part of us that we manage to keep quiet during the day, and does what it wants. The night is its realm. And it is a realm of freedom.

I have a habit of holding my dreams in high regard, of paying attention to them, of noting the most important ones in a notebook and trying to process them, not so much as a psychoanalytic practice but as if they were fragments left behind by my nocturnal self precisely so that I can put those pieces back together.

Exercise no. 3

Start giving importance to your dreams and call your nocturnal self when you go to sleep. We can take a concrete action, such as putting a glass of water on the bedside table and drinking half of it before we fall asleep and the remainder when we wake up, or we can say a sentence as we close our eyes: "Let me remember my dream" or "I open myself to the images that will come in my dreams tonight." And keep a journal and a pen handy to write the dreams down when you wake up. A few words will do, just enough to remember the crucial parts; we can write the whole thing down later.

Apart from how to interpret dreams, when we write them down, let's try not to think: "It's probably just some byproduct of my brain," "I dreamt of falling; it's not a big deal, everyone does." Let's not be superficial: Give dreams importance, respect them. Otherwise we will do the same with our intuitions, with ideas that come from above, we will sit there thinking, "It doesn't mean anything." Instead, let's treat the unexplainable as if it were a treasure; let's jump in, let's do anything to relate to it. We have to start thinking, "I don't understand it, I can't explain it, and that's exactly why it's so important and wonderful."

Ambush no. 3

It's okay to be afraid to dream. To lie in bed and think, "Oh god, what will the other me see tonight?" To feel that we are at the mercy of a limitless ocean in which we are about to drown, overtaken by a storm. That is precisely the feeling we need to experience when confronted with our feminine: to recognize that we are in the presence of a powerful force that is a part of us but it is the part that does not want to be controlled like a monkey.

A friend of mine who used to come to intùiti nights hadn't dreamt in over a decade. That was the first thing she told me. She was so afraid of what she would see at night that she blocked everything out, stopped remembering the dreams she had, both the bad ones and the good ones. How could she be creative, holding herself back like that? When she dared to be afraid and delved into them, she started dreaming again, and the quality of her work improved.

We must dare to push ourselves, to go right where we are most afraid of going, and if it is our irrational part that terrifies us, we must have the courage to lose control and be completely authentic.

If you do not lose control, you will only be half creative. You will write intelligent manuals, well-constructed books, and sensible, well-thought works of art, and you even may be able to make good plans. But there will never be that extra something in there.

The soul will not be there.

4) Brainopening and stream of consciousness

Last year, I made it a point to write every morning—even for just ten minutes, to light a candle and write. At first it was "easier" because I had a novel to finish and another one to work on right after, so I knew what direction to move in; I had a task and a goal. Some days I wrote more, some days less, but all in all, it worked. When I finished the novels, I felt self-conscious. What the hell was I going to write? I would look at the blank page and think, "What am I going to do now? How do those superproductive writers like Stephen King do it?" For a few weeks, I wrote fairy tales, one a day; I'd stand there in front of the computer, or I'd walk around the kitchen with a coffee in my hand, and something would come along, and I'd put it down. After about fifteen of those, I realized I was losing interest; I felt like I was doing a school assignment, a design project. It was similar to what I had been doing at the beginning of my advertising career, when I was a copywriter and had to write little stories for Parmalat S.p.A., an Italian dairy and food corporation.

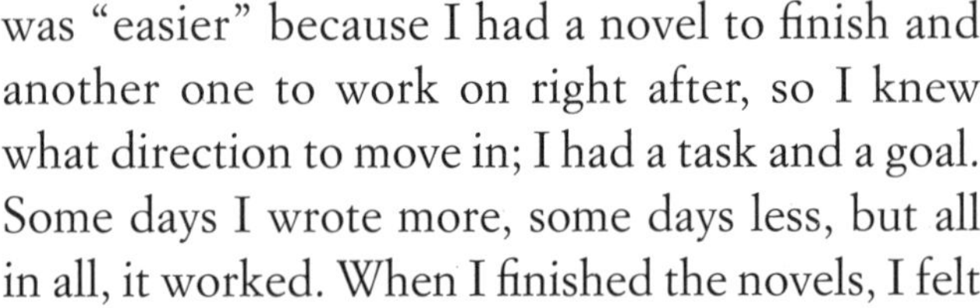

I talked to my teacher about it, and she said, "Try writing in a stream of consciousness. Sit there and see what comes out."

I immediately frowned. I thought, "Jeez, what am I going to do with all those random words piled up there anyway? What is it? A kid's journal? What kind of bullshit is this?"

The one who was talking and resisting was my masculine, who was willing to devote time every morning to writing but only if it came with tangible results. It's one thing to write a novel, another to throw sentences and periods on a piece of paper. Can you grasp the difference? Writing for the sheer sake of writing and experimenting, or for the desire to have material to publish. Eventually, I decided to leave the mumbling masculine aside and rely on the feminine, and I did that for almost three months. I jotted down more than forty thousand words (the length of a short novel) of absurd, sometimes weird or grotesque images. I would start with sounds that came into my head as soon as I woke up; it might be a whoosh, a roar, a bray, a rapture, and I would go after them, building words and sentences in a rush, and then stories that would slide across the screen before I could think them through. Without realizing it, I would slip in scenes and names from books I was reading or movies I had seen, or things that had happened the night before. Some pieces were loaded with anger that I needed to throw out, others with hope or energy. I was putting it all in the hands of another me who knew what to do; it was a bit like dreaming.

After a month and a half, the images began to change. I could feel an upward connection, something that must have always been there but that I was grasping poorly before and now I finally got it. Scenes of divine battles, of different dimensions, of Lucifer talking to St. Anne in the hills of Turin. At first, I just jotted them down, and little by little, I realized that they were related to each other, that they were part of the same world. Eventually, I understood that they were inspirations for the sequel to a fantasy book I had written the year before and didn't know how to continue.

Thanks to those images, I picked up the project again and finished it in five months. And I would never have been able to do it without that exercise. Where did those inspirations come from?

Who knows?

I do the same out loud—let's call it a *brainopening* instead of brainstorming: I walk back and forth around the house, or in a park, or at the coffee shop, alone or with colleagues, partners, friends, and try to enjoy myself as I let the associations come, not as achievements that I have to find at all costs but as pearls that descend from above. To help myself, I imagine a channel coming into my head, and I just focus on trying to be open and free to let the channel reach me.

I did that to write this book as well. After the second chapter, I got stuck and I thought, "I don't know how to go on, and what I've put down so far is just shit." So I grabbed my notebook, I imagined that I had to get some creativity lectures ready for school, and I jotted down the titles of each lecture. Starting from there, I spoke for three days at home alone to an imaginary audience, and as I did so, I found that the words came on their own. More importantly, I felt that I was finding the right tone within my own voice, a way to talk about creativity and to inspire and instigate it. I didn't even take notes of the strange things I said alone in my living room. I just opened up, and the rest came flowing in.

Exercise no. 4

Let's play a game: For seven days, at the same time of each day, write what pops into your mind. It can be in the morning, afternoon, or evening, whenever you want. Sit there and let it flow freely. If you skip a day, start over from day one. You can write it down, which will leave tangible proof on paper, or you can walk back and forth and record yourself talking out loud. You can even start by complaining, saying, "Oh my god, what am I doing?"

Oh my god, what am I doing? I feel like an idiot talking and writing without purpose. Why am I doing this when I have a million things to do, like what, ah I don't know, I can't think of any, oh well, good for you, I could cook, I'm craving chicken today, I could roast it with some yams, but olives, ah I don't have any, damn, it'll taste like nothing without olives.

I don't like tasteless things, lukewarm things are boring, like this foggy day. Could it be a mirror? Am I the lukewarm and boring one? The paleness gets a hold of me, there's too much light, but the sun is beyond. I would like to be a bird: Maybe they do it, they soar above and fly in the sun to get over this boredom and this grayness.

Go ahead and allow yourself to feel unashamed of the silly things you write. You don't need to read it twice; just get used to the freedom of expression and embrace the experience of something that might be an idea you haven't fully explored. The image of a bird flying beyond the fog came to me unexpectedly. If I had focused on it, I probably wouldn't have come up with it. We can revisit this exercise whenever we feel pressured to perform. If we're pushing ourselves too hard or worried about finding the right idea, we can take some time to let go and embrace the irrational to see what comes out of it. As mentioned earlier, this is the method I used to write this book.

5) Creativity without performance

One of the first things my teacher asks you to do once you start working with her is an oil painting: a self-portrait or an image that you feel in your kundalini (the vital force), or a picture of your spirit animal (if you have already found yours). Everyone has some resistance at first: "I don't know how to paint," "I've never done it." "It's not important what the painting looks like," she answers. "It is important that you do it."

I did my first self-portrait out of spite, like usual. She said, "Do you feel like doing it today?" Of course, I didn't feel like doing it, and I also thought that it was a stupid request, but I said to myself, "I'm not going to be the one who backs out." I still have it hanging on the wall in my home along with the rest of the self-portraits that I have painted throughout the years. While I painted for the first time, I realized two things: First is that I had zero interest in being a painter—it meant nothing to me; second, that the result was significant, real, and tangible—I was making an object, like a mug or a statue, and this object claimed its place in space. If I had to create a logo of myself, as a designer I wouldn't feel completely free. The same goes if I had to write the story of my life. On the other hand, with painting, it's okay if the shading is not perfect. Even if it comes out bad, it's all right; it makes me feel I can be more fluid in creating. The performance is not crucial; the representation, the appearance of the work and its intent are. One time I showed a picture of one of my paintings to a somewhat famous artist who said, with a bit of disdain in his voice: "It is clear that there is no technique." And I was surprised by the fact that I didn't take it personally; I actually kept on looking at the screen with pride, as if he had just paid me a compliment.

To me, that painting was important for a whole different reason. The lack of performance gives enormous freedom. We will never judge ourselves in respect to an art form in which we have no interest to excel (if you are painters, of course, you are going to need to find a different example!), and this allows us to express ourselves free of restraints, without worrying. The worst that can happen is that we toss everything and we do it all over again, or we can cover it and paint over it or we keep it the way it came out the first time since we don't have to show it to anybody.

I firmly believe this is the way through which our feminine can give us gifts; it can give us something that we will never know where it came from. For me it happened with a self-portrait of myself, which came out as a bizarre character in red, blue, and yellow, somewhere between a cat and a demon, and it became the cover of *Mario*, the novel I cherish the most. Even more remarkable is the painting I did in China when I lived there. One evening I went up to the roof and painted the skyline, and in the end, overcome by nostalgia, I added my cat looking at the horizon. Well, Sefirot's logo is really a vector of that image.

Giving this kind of freedom to our feminine is a proper rebellion against the masculine that has been programmed to desire grades and results.

Exercise no. 5

Let's buy canvases, brushes, and some oil or acrylic colors (white, black, and the three primaries—red, blue, and yellow—from which we can make all colors). Don't wait for a week. Do it today or tomorrow at the latest. Let's take a mirror and paint ourselves, or let's paint one of the dreams we've had lately, or, since we've talked about it so much, let's paint our feminine side, as we envision it. Let the brush run across the canvas and see where it takes us, as if it were an extension of our arm. Perhaps our feminine side will emerge like a blinding sun, or like a cat coming out of a tree. Let your body guide you instinctively.

We can repeat this exercise as many times as we want, even as a culmination or summary of other exercises in the book. Over time, it can help us build a real imagery of who we are and what we feel, an imagery that we can hang on the walls of our home or office, a reference for self reflection.

**For painters: You can do this exercise trying to just let go, to forget about technique; or, if you can't, try to do the exercise using clay, or drawing with a pen, or writing and keeping the page as if it were a painting.*

On the left, self-portrait used as *Mario*'s cover (2018).

On the right, painting of my kundalini (2020).

On the left, painting of Shenzhen skyline with imagined cat (2016).

On the bottom, Sefirot's logo.

6) Using irrational tools

When facing difficulties, I use intùiti face down; I draw the cards that attract me, and I let the images and their meanings inspire me. If I don't know whether I want to end the chapter of the novel one way or the other, I draw a card with the intention of being provoked by the corresponding archetype. "Cut," suggests the card, or "This is good," or "There's something you're not telling yourself." How does it make me feel? On the right track or the wrong track? How do I react when faced with an irrational urge?

Example: I have to choose whether to accept a job or not, and I have made the list of pros and cons but I feel that it is not enough to make me choose. I might draw a card, surrender for a moment, and indulge in a completely reckless act. Imagine this: You are standing in front of the place where you are supposed to sign the contract. You already have the appointment, but you are not sure, so you walk into the coffee shop across the street, get a coffee, take out your deck of intùiti, shuffle it, and draw a card under the eyes of the bartender who looks at you funny. Ha ha. And the card that comes up punches you in the gut. "You're only doing it for the money," it whispers, or it makes you think, "You don't like that company, you hate it," or worse, it tells you, "Run as fast as you can!" What if it suggested doing something completely different? If it showed a bright and peaceful image? What if it said, "This is exactly your path"? In other words, how would it make you feel to receive an irrational nudge?

Imagine being there, sitting at the café being completely unsure about what to do, when you start staring at the blue and black card you drew and you realize that you don't want that job. There are more pros than cons, but the no is suddenly so strong (and you don't know how to explain it!), so you simply walk away. You call the person you had the appointment with, tell them that you have reconsidered, and poof, you walk away.

This is the feminine manifesting itself: There is definitely a reason to go to the right instead of to the left, but we don't know how to put it into words. Tools like intùiti are there to stir the waters, to give us little shocks, epiphanies. It's not a spell: When we try to make rational decisions, we are, in fact, silencing our feminine (which already knows what we really want to do), and sometimes all it takes is a little nudge to get it talking again.

After the first call with Studiolabo, the company that would become a creative partner in the creation of BAD Canvas, I was very much against working with them. I was offended because I felt a vibe similar to the one I had suffered years earlier at the Milan Polytechnic: a bit snobbish, uptight, and I decided to be an ass. My partner at the time pointed out to me that I was having a disproportionate and baseless reaction; so I drew an intùiti card and out came the XVIII, a very proud sun, and I felt clearly that I had a great desire to work on that project. That was good, because BAD is one of the tools I am most fond of. Would I have done it even if another card had come out?

Well, another card didn't come out. Ha ha.

Exercise no. 6

Let's try using an irrational tool to prod us on a specific choice. Don't know whether to work on a project? Whether to change jobs, cities, partners? Whether to go to an event this evening? Whether to go to our parents' for dinner? It can be anything.

You can use intùiti, if you have them, or tarot cards, or *I Ching*, or dice, or you can even toss a coin. Let's rely for a moment on something that we don't know and can't know; let's get out of reality whereby everything is defined by your will, and if you succeed, it's your own merit, and if you fail, it's your fault, and me, me, me, me. How boring. We experience reality, which is also made up of luck and coincidences, strange alignments, hunches, and unexplainable feelings that change our lives and, in hindsight, change them in the right way.

Come on, let's dare for once. Let's experience the thrill of trusting the unknown. Let's flip a coin, draw a card.

Woooooo.

How did that make you feel?

**Frequently asked question: "Do I have to follow what the card or the coin that I tossed says?"*

No, you are always the compass. You must recognize how it made you feel to receive a random response. For example, you might flip a coin as to whether or not to go to an event, hoping it comes up tails (don't go), and then notice, when it comes up heads (go), that you are strangely relieved and suddenly have a great urge to get the car and get out. Or you could experiment—actually follow a random response and see what happens. Does the coin tell you to go even though you don't feel like it? Do it anyway and see what happens! Maybe you'll get a pleasant surprise.

Conclusions

These exercises are about getting acquainted with the feminine side, about experiencing what it is and what the difference is between brainopening and brainstorming, between striving to come up with ideas at all costs and letting something come to you spontaneously.

They are important so that we do not fall into misunderstandings with the feminine, which, I am going to say it one more time: It is not only the grace of a receptive cup, but is also the exuberance of the unknown, a force that cannot be controlled and that might catch us off guard and make us want to get up from a dinner party and run away (and she would almost certainly be right!).

For those already familiar with the feminine, it will be easier, but the idea behind these exercises is to get us used to holding an uncontrollable power and trusting it. Gradually, we will realize that we have more intuition, at all times, and that we will no longer be afraid to follow it, even giving up doing what we are doing and what seemed so important, to find that intuition leads us toward a quicker solution. We will feel like leaving the house to have coffee, to keep writing instead of stopping, to take a break, to be whimsical instead of judicious, to have fun.

Let's not worry if we do it clumsily at first, if we go along with the intuition too late and lose momentum, or if we go along with it for too long and feel inefficient. We are not perfect—we are not machines—and that is exactly what our feminine wants to teach us.

Train the masculine side

Our feminine alone is not enough. It is a vital part, but if it is not channeled, that drive will be unable to come to fruition. We have already made the example of Gregory, who has a thousand ideas and cannot follow through on even one of them and, in the grip of a kind of excessive euphoria, talks about them again and again. That is a symptom of a lack of the masculine, of a lack of action toward a definite path, toward saying, "Okay, I like this one, I am going to pursue it." Every time we feel like we are procrastinating, that we have no discipline, that we are getting zero done, our masculine is not pushing us the right way. Go back to the image on page 111: The feminine helps us fill the cup, but it is the masculine that decides what intuition to bring forward and pursue. In the masculine, we find responsibility, keeping our feet firm on the ground: "I am going to do it." It is the bridge between the up and down, between the idea and reality. The feminine tends to fly a bit too high, so it needs the masculine to stay within reality.

Among the products I have developed at Sefirot, there are two that seem diametrically opposite: intùiti is a tool for working on yourself and your intuitions (very feminine), and BAD is a framework for designing with business aspects in mind, which helps make a project really stand on its feet (extremely masculine). Sometimes at conferences or presentations, someone raises their hand to say, "But how is it that after developing a product like intùiti, you do something as mundane"—they say *mundane* even though they would like to use the word *petty*—"as BAD?"

The answer is that you need both worlds.

With intùiti, a person can open up and let the idea of a big project come, but to carry it out, that same person needs a structured method like BAD. We need great openness as well as strong and decisive action to turn our idea into something real, achievable, and accomplished. The feeling and the action. The magic and the discipline.

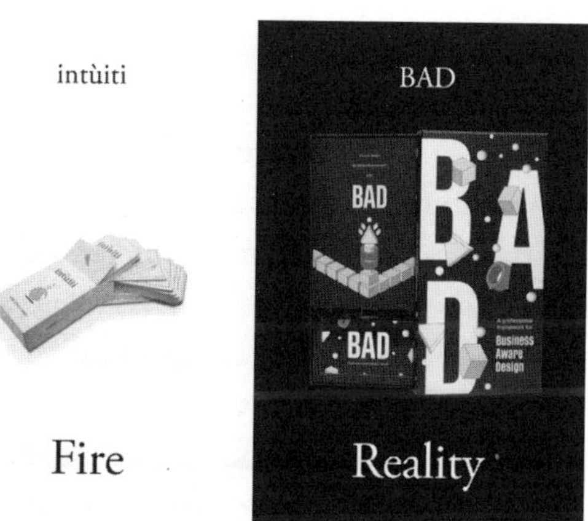

I would never have accomplished anything if I had merely felt the ideas coming. And the feeling is a moment, a tiny glimpse, a brief burst of lightning. What comes next requires constant determination and will, day after day. The flash of intùiti lasted a few seconds, but the work on the cards went on for almost two years. For a good four months, I would go to the library every morning and work all day on the creation of each individual card, its meanings and how to convey its messages. The same thing happened with every other project—with Fabula, Cicero, with the company itself—but also with the novels: It can't be a heroic furor every day, every hour, every moment. It takes the will to put yourself out there for a fixed time, and do it. And today it will be good, tomorrow it will be bad, one moment it will be wow, the next it will be shit, but in the end, you will get to a result.

I remember a speech by writer and actor Ethan Hawke, who was talking about his screenwriting process: "If I were to write only when I'm inspired," he explained, "I would never write. I sit at the table and then inspiration comes."

Hemingway wrote early in the morning, at fixed hours; so did the Marquis de Sade, from seven to ten at night. Henry Miller, having spent half his life in the grip of his feminine side—writing carried away by momentum—said that his life changed (and his output improved) when he began writing for only three hours in the morning.

When we throw ourselves out of bed to go for a run, that's the masculine. When we strive to work late into the night so as not to miss a deadline, that is, once again, the masculine. Organization, sense of duty, willpower, discipline. When used well, it gives great support to the feminine, because it paves the way for her, creates space for her to work, makes sure that we're sitting at our desks from seven to nine to write, so that when and if the feminine wants to inspire us, we will be ready.

The masculine also forces us to come to terms with reality, to size up our dreams and actions so that there is no gap between them. The masculine is the one that, without fuss, tells us, "If you really want to write that book, sit down and write it."

Training system for strengthening the masculine

Each of us has one part more developed than the other (men often have a stronger masculine and women a more developed feminine). If you have found the exercises to train the feminine hard, it should be easier to do the exercises that train the masculine, and vice versa.

The following exercises are meant to shock those who are less organized and fall into procrastination, or to those who believe that inspiration must necessarily need a free and unregulated space. We will see that this is not the case.

1) Eight hours a day

A graphic designer friend of mine told me that she could not be productive enough. "I work a lot," she said, "but in the end, I'm always tired and not focused enough."

I asked her what her daily routine was, and she explained that she woke up when she felt like, she started working around 10:00 a.m., even 10:30 a.m., and she would keep going until late at night, taking breaks—sometimes long ones—during the day. "In the morning, I don't feel creative," she said, "but I do at night."

"Why don't you try this," I told her. "Come to my office from 9:00 a.m. to 6:00 p.m. Not one minute more. You take a one hour lunch break and that's it."

"But I just told you I'm not creative in the morning!" she complained.

I burst out laughing, "You are actually scared of working!"

She nodded, looking guilty, and she never even tried following my advice.

I learned how to work when I lived in the Netherlands, between 2012 and 2014. I was a designer for a digital agency. Work started at 9:30 a.m., we had a half-hour lunch break at

12.30 p.m. when we would eat a sandwich, and at 6 p.m. sharp, everyone was out of there. Sometimes I'd check the time at 6:03 p.m., realizing I'd gotten distracted—and everyone at the desks beside me was already gone. During those years, I learned about my productive capability and what I can create in eight hours. In the Dutch agency, there were no meetings: The project manager would come to you and explain what you had to do, and you did it. There was no procrastination, because no one felt like staying one minute longer than the allotted time.

You might think that it was not a creative environment, that a lack of long hours and meetings made the work less creative. But instead, I had to change my mind: I was unstoppable, I designed some cool stuff, had some amazing ideas, and I did it with unparalleled efficiency and speed.

We love the idea of working late, of playing the part of the bohemian artist sitting in a dark attic (I was in love with that for years), but when you try to follow schedules, the result is shocking. I remember thinking, "If I had worked like this in college, I would have finished my thesis in five weeks." And it was a pretty accurate estimation.

Exercise no. 1

For one week, let's try to experiment with a well-organized work schedule, which could translate to working eight hours a day without wasting too much time and making sure you finish by 6:00 p.m.–6:30 p.m.

If you are a freelancer or an entrepreneur, that means setting specific hours, from nine to six. We don't go to the gym on our lunch break; we go in the evening, after work, or before we start in the morning. Nine to six, no excuses.

If you are an employee and your work schedule is already pretty much that, try for a week not to waste time. As a former employee, I understand the challenges—we shouldn't take numerous long cigarette or coffee breaks, or spend excessive time on social media or texting friends. It's essential to make the most of our time and be efficient to realize our full potential within the eight-hour workday. Just imagine the possibilities if we allocate two hours each day for activities we enjoy! Amazing, right?

2) Wake up at dawn

In 2021, I was following a Hermetic Qabalah journey developed by Kristos T. Perry involving particular exercises and tasks divided in twenty-eight-day cycles, and for one month, I had to wake up at dawn. A few minutes before dawn, to be exact. I am a morning person, but not to that extreme, so I will spare you the swearing that went on. By the way, it was almost summer, so every day the alarm clock rang sooner and sooner. If I started the month by waking up at 7:10 a.m., I ended it by getting up at 6:20 a.m.

I was not used to that time slot where the sky is dark, the city is not quite awake, and the employees are still in bed. I was having coffee, going to the bathroom, and it was barely 7:30 a.m. "What do I do now?" I wondered. Eventually, I decided that I would use that time to work on a new novel, so every morning, I would wake up, go to the office, and write for almost two hours before "officially" starting my day.

At the end of the month, the whole foundation of the novel was there.

Exercise no. 2

Let's try to wake up before dawn each day (or, if you already do, an hour earlier). And in that time we've carved out, let's dedicate ourselves to something we truly want: writing, drawing, reading, working on a board game, studying, learning a language. Whatever. It will cost us effort; we will be tired, have dark circles under our eyes, and in the evening, we will not feel like doing anything. But let's try it for a week and observe how our mood changes, what happens to us, and, especially, what we manage to do in that extra time.

Ambush no. 4

But I can't be creative on command! But I need my own time, and blah, blah, blah. Wah, wah, wah. You don't know if it's true unless you try it. You have to get out of your comfort zone without excuses and without bugging yourself and others. These exercises should not become the norm. I do not wake up every morning at dawn nor do I always work eight hours like a robot. I know what my work capacity is, though. I know what I can achieve if I want to. And I know that if I put in two hours a day doing something, ideas come and the project slowly builds.

If you don't do these exercises, however, you will never have this awareness. You will continue to complain, or worse, wallow in the thought: "I wish I could but I don't have the time."

There is no such thing as time; you can stretch it and build it as you see fit. And the sooner you have this experience, the sooner you will realize it.

3) Create space to create

We have been bombarded by the idealist-creative-bohemian notion that great creativity comes from the great mess, the image of the room with books scattered on the floor, the mad artist's cave, and so on. In my twenties, I lived that way. I ate like a college student, cooking myself terrible pasta dishes, and I would then leave the dirty plates in the sink for several days as I went back and forth around the house working on a variety of projects. I was sloppy in the name of creativity. When I launched intùiti's Kickstarter campaign, my kitchen was in shameful conditions. I was unorganized, I was doing everything half-assed, fidgeting and getting angry, and I was convinced that I had to indulge my whim, my intuition.

I wanted something that I was passionate about to wake me up (or even to keep me up) that would keep me sitting on that chair to write.

I was, in fact, convinced that rules and discipline were only good for work, for what I did in the office and what fed me. But privately, I hated it and yearned for the poetry of creative coitus, of the uncontrollable force of genius. Ha ha. When I entered the house, I lived as a beggar of sorts waiting for inspiration. I wasn't sitting at my desk saying, "Okay, let's make room for creativity." I was living at the mercy of my feminine. I was waiting for the urge, almost as if it was a sin to do anything if I had not first heard the muse knocking at my door.

In hindsight, it wasn't entirely the wrong approach—just a risky one. Being inside the hurricane all the time, looking forward to the storm on clear days, was intense, but it was leading me toward exhaustion, just like living in a constantly filthy room after a while makes you want to burn everything down and change apartments. And above all, I was living on a nerve-racking roller coaster, made up of months of wows and months of boredom and nostalgia for the wows I felt before. So, was I really more creative?

Around the age of thirty, I started taking better care of my space, cleaning up the table before I got down to writing or working, sweeping the floor and picking up the cups and glasses I had a habit of leaving everywhere. I also began to allow myself time to create without always having to wait for inspiration. Without realizing it, I was preparing the space for creativity.

The most shocking surprise was realizing how feminine and masculine could work together. When I decided that I would work on my new novel every day, there were mornings when I was a machine, writing two, three thousand words, and other mornings when I paced back and forth drinking one coffee after another, unable to really write anything. Those were some magical days: After two hours of discomfort and frustration, here would come a page or two toward the end of the morning that needed to be written out of the blue, and there I was, ready to seize it.

It was hard to admit that I had better insights while sitting in my chair like in an office and not walking down the street or going for a run, as my damned poet ideal suggested.

Exercise no. 3

Let's create space for creativity. Every morning, set aside time for something you truly want to do—and see what happens. Let's drop all the excuses and justifications and simply get on with doing. And let's not worry about issues like: "But I don't like this way," "I don't want to work this way." It is an experience. Let's do it and then see how we feel and what really works for us.

The goal is to really get out of the comfort zone (which, as I mentioned above, can also be a discomfort zone, but that is the only one we are used to), and discover a new way of experiencing creativity.

Repetition is the death of creativity; it is the pattern that keeps us anchored in habits that are always the same and that block our cues and make us old. So let's break the patterns: Let's go work at the coffee shop, tomorrow at the library, or on the couch, in the bedroom, at the train station. Who said you can't write a book during a plane ride while the guy next to you keeps reading what you're writing? Let's try it! Ha ha. Maybe he is an editor and will give us his card.

I've been doing the same things

for the past twenty years.

The same ol' turning wheel

because that's how I function.

What a bore.

4) Choose what to work on

Reading the points mentioned above, someone may have wondered, "Well, I can commit to work on something but . . . on what?" That's it! To pursue an idea, one must necessarily choose one. At this exact moment (Thursday, December 14 at 9:18 a.m.), I have the following ideas: designing a new payment system for Sefirot's website; fixing the second volume of the fantasy book I wrote; reviewing *Mario5*, the fifth book of the *Mario* saga; developing a tool to process dreams; launching a new company branch focused on consulting and changing the business model on my old UXBox project. And these are just the practical ones. (If I were to freewheel it I could go on and on and on, ha ha.)

All the ideas I have mentioned, which may sound grand, are actually still nothing. They are just ideas, glowing balls arrived from above, Plato's noumenon, an intangible something that can inspire me, but they simply do not exist yet. To make them real, I have to choose to reach out and pull the idea down to earth; for example, open a Word file and say, "Now I am going to work on this," knowing that it is not going to be something I can finish in ten minutes but a journey that could be one, two, six months long. Performing that first action takes tremendous energy and will continue to ask for energy until the project is done.

When I decide to start something, I know there is no going back. The moment right before the start is solemn: I feel that I am about to commit myself to an undertaking that will be with me for some time and from which I will not be able to escape easily. If I start writing a book, then I cannot just throw down a couple of pages and leave it there: The book has now entered reality and it will stay in the room and stare at me.

Our masculine side does just that: It takes something and brings it into reality. It is the will to do. We cross the threshold that lies between the world of imagination and the concrete world hand in hand with our idea, which from now on immediately takes shape and becomes a real project. It requires energy and responsibility, because once we bring it to this side, then we are required to actually construct it; we can no longer look at the idea from a safe distance, basking in its enormous potential.

We open ourselves up to possible failure: not being able to accomplish what we wanted to do, or not being able to do it the way we imagined. In short, we are putting ourselves on the line and running the risk of feeling inconclusive or, worse, incompetent.

And there is no solution to this discomfort. We must know that this is exactly how we might feel. That is exactly the courage we must have. Do you think that even after so many successful projects I don't feel that way every time? Do you think your idols whose books you have read or whose works you have admired have not felt this way? Don't be naive: Even the greatest creative feels this way deep down. And they still dive into the creative act, thanks to willpower: They dare to risk failing.

Every time I start a new project, I think that it might turn out to be a disaster and that I might feel terrible for giving up in the middle or for not being able to do it. And, well, I do it anyway.

It's a high price to pay, and it warns us against deciding to follow the first idea that comes to mind and losing time over it. I think about it ten times before I start a new project, because investing all that energy has to be worth it. Really, really worth it.

**Frequently asked question: "What if I'm not the one choosing the project? If it is assigned from a client or my boss?"*

In that case, which is the most common case in the work environment, especially if you work in an agency or design studio, our responsibility is considerably reduced. We are not the ones who put in the willpower and choose the project, so the stakes are lower. Deep down, we don't care too much about the success of the project: It might even turn out to be a small professional failure, but not a personal one. The intensity is entirely different. If we submit a project to win a competition with a client and that client chooses another agency, we may get upset, but it is not a tragedy; if, on the other hand, we reread our manuscript and realize that we failed to convey what we wanted, the disappointment is scorching.

This is why I always encourage those who have never pursued a personal project to do so: to feel the change of pace and the drastic increase in focus that follows.

Exercise no. 4

Pick an idea and define the starting point of you actively working on that idea. For example:

- Buy a new notebook and start jotting down the structure of your novel.
- Take a note of the things we need to launch the project that we've been thinking about for a while.
- Grab paper and a pencil and sketch the logo of the company we would like to open.
- Design the first pieces of clothing for our clothing collection.
- Order the books we need to do research for the essay we want to write.

- Start sending résumés to companies we are interested in, if we want to change jobs.

And, most importantly, take this first step with the knowledge and responsibility to not go back.

I don't send out résumés just for the sake of it; I don't stop until I get a job. I don't start writing a book just for fun as if I'm writing two pages in the diary and then that's it; I must start being pushed by a very strong desire to get it done. And that goes for any project.

Otherwise, don't start. Pause for a moment and think. Ask yourself whether it is really necessary to do it and whether you feel ready. If the answer is no, it is better to wait. I have been pondering a new edition of intùiti for years, but I have never started. There is nothing wrong with that, just be aware.

5) Determine yourself

In one of the agencies I worked for, one of the creative directors was the quintessential alpha male. He had a habit of

explaining what he wanted, and then placing his fist on the table as he reiterated, "I want it done 120 percent." He didn't slam the fist—he just placed it on the surface—but it felt like a hammer hitting the table. We laughed about it endlessly in the office; we made so much fun of him, but it did get the message across: He was stubborn, headstrong, determined. "While I'm working here," he told me one day, "I will give it my 120 percent."

When I was about to flee Milan to go to Amsterdam, my teacher told me, "Try to stay there for at least a year. Make it a point to do so. Don't give in right away." In other words: Feel everything that comes up, but be determined and don't give up.

Our masculine side doesn't listen, and it does so in the most boorish way: “Now that I said it, I’d rather die than not do it,” “The math adds up so what I predicted must happen,” “I promised I am not going to move from here until I am done,” “It is a matter of honor: I must do it.” That pure stubbornness can help us stand on our feet while the storm is raging. In wartime, I would want someone like that creative director by my side, who bangs his fist on the table and shouts, “If I decide to fight, I fight giving it 120 percent!”

Once we felt the idea, and we decided to work on it, we need the part of us that doesn’t give up.

When I had finished drawing intùiti, I made a very first production of fifty pieces and started using them at my teacher’s restaurant in downtown Milan. I would go there a couple of times a week, have a glass of wine, and pester the patrons asking if they wanted to try intùiti. After a couple of months, I got demoralized; I felt like I was just standing there wasting my time, and I started skipping appointments. My teacher noticed that I wasn’t going anymore, and one night, I got the very first ambush of my life.

We were smoking a cigarette and she asked me, “Why don’t you come over anymore?” I answered, “Nothing ever happens. I’m tired.” I thought she would agree since she often told me that I shouldn’t do what I didn’t feel like doing, yet that evening she caught me off guard. “Lino told me that you were the quitting type.” She looked serious, she stared at me harshly. Lino was the professor who connected us. “He said, ‘Don’t waste your time with him, he’s a quitter.’ I answered that I didn’t agree. But it seems like he was right. You have a good project in your hands, and you are giving up like this.”

I felt my face become hot and swollen, and in my ears, I heard a sharp, unbearable ringing. I wanted to kill her because she had dared to call me weak, and mostly because I felt that she was right, and I wanted to crush the small table between us, and the chairs, and the couch, to show that I had the strength to carry out whatever I put my mind to.

After that night, I started going to the restaurant again (I did it unwillingly, because I felt like a pain in the ass, but I did it), and I continued to do the same after I moved to Amsterdam: I found cafés that would accommodate me, and I started bothering people with my cards.

I never actually gained anything from those evenings; I did not meet a publisher who said, “Wow, I am going to publish this,” nor did I gain any interesting contacts to develop the project. I did gain a (precious) friend and a couple of free drinks, but mostly I learned to be stubborn, to keep going undeterred even if I felt ashamed. I learned to become like a nail that won’t come out under any circumstances—I learned how to be determined.

My teacher used to tell me, “Maybe only one person will show up at the first presentation. You’ll get two at the second one, at your third, you’ll get three, and so on.” What matters in the end, and it took me years to understand this, is to learn how to still hold the presentation even if no one showed up. To work for Sefirot is not always fun—I can guarantee it. Opening a company, managing staff, dealing with bureaucratic issues, worrying about sales, finding new business models, and so on.

You have to want it so badly that you plant your feet on the ground, banish hatchets, guns, and whatnot, and break out your fingernails. It doesn’t just take intuition, the idea, the passion; it also takes determination, that thing where everyone looks at you thinking from time to time, “Who’s forcing him to keep going?,” and the answer is: “Me. I want to go down this road so much that I’m ready to do anything.”

Exercise no. 5

We have chosen something to work on; we worked hard, and we were consistent. Now let's make a commitment, not a promise ("I'm going to write a book" . . . but when???), which is totally useless to us right now. What we want is a real commitment, a less dreamy and more concrete, powerful sentence, one that makes us emotional as we say it out loud.

Take a piece of paper and write:

- *I commit to write a book, and I will not stop until it is finished.*
- *I pledge to open my business and keep it open for at least one year.*
- *I pledge to paint one painting a week for twenty weeks.*

Create your own commitment and stand by it, bang your fist on the table, and remember: "If I do something, I do it by giving it my 120 percent!"

Conclusions

These exercises help us understand the value of our masculine side: the drive to take action, to initiate, and to engage in daily activities in a practical and mindful way. The exercises also teach us to honor the grumpy part of us, the stubborn, obstinate, and even a little obtuse parts that we tend to forget about when it comes to creativity.

If your masculine side is untrained, you may have difficulty with the exercises above; you may feel constrained and frustrated. In that case, there is no need to overdo it: What is important is to start experimenting with your masculine side and find out how far you can push it and what its characteristics and attitudes are.

Those whose feminine side is overdeveloped will have to make a greater effort to ground themselves in reality; those who are too rigid will have to try to open up as much as possible, be more undisciplined, more whimsical.

Each of us is wired differently, depending on the time and era of our lives. There is no definite rule, no absolute right and wrong. Sometimes it will be better to put our heads down and work for ten hours straight, other times the solution is to get up and run, to freak out, to be unpredictable.

For now, let's try to be mindful of the two different vibes: one that encourages us to let go and feel free, and another that empowers us to bring our feelings into reality.

Internal critics

We have already said that life is neither an equation nor a binary series of zeroes and ones, and neither is creativity. As wonderful as the ideal of yin and yang perfection is, reality does not work with the same geometric precision. On the contrary, the creative process is absolutely nonlinear; we can imagine it as a thread being stirred up by a storm of masculine and feminine tossing us left and right.

Let's look at Jennifer: Tonight she comes home and has an epiphany. She sees the first scene of her novel, and wow, caught up in the momentum, she cancels the meeting she had with her friend and she writes until two o'clock in the morning putting down, about ten pages; the next day she decides that she will continue every night, but when she gets home from work, she is too tired, so she decides to watch a movie on her laptop; the next day, same thing, and so the next, until Saturday when she looks in the mirror and remembers, "You want to be a writer. Then write." She writes for nine days straight, at least two hours a day, getting the first five chapters down. She feels very proud of herself, until one morning when she feels like throwing it all away because she feels the story sucks; it is not as powerful as in those first ten pages.

Maybe she just wanted to write a short story . . . maybe she forced herself into something that is not for her . . .

The storm that is overtaking Jennifer will get stronger and stronger until she finishes the first draft of the novel which will happen in fifteen months. Fun, right? Ha ha.

The same happens to all of us. At this point, you have learned how to feel the influences of the masculine (the authoritarian voice saying, "You have to do it every day!") and the feminine vibes ("I don't like it today, let's change everything!"). These two influences work as internal critics, and they will torment us the entire time, so we must learn how to coexist with them and to understand when it is right to listen and when it is necessary to push them away a little.

First of all, remember that it is normal: All creatives feel the same. I will repeat it until I drop. Don't let the positive thinking trend bring you down. The whole "It's all good, it's all amazing" mindset isn't true—everything moves within polarity: good and bad, easy and hard, high and low. If we strive to feel our creativity, to do big things and fly high, we must accept to open the door to the abyss. As above so below. Put your heart to rest: Everyone feels like we do. Even the greatest. We are not alone. Don't get dramatic and learn to dive deep into this intensity. What we should look at is when to pay attention to our feminine critic and when to pay attention to the masculine critic.

Let's get Jennifer involved once more. We said that the ideal would be to let the feminine get us in tune with our intuitions, and then the masculine can help us to have the necessary consistency to develop them so we can move into a virtuous circle made of idea and action, idea and action. Unfortunately at one point, the circle breaks and one of the two—masculine or feminine—raises its hand and its voice.

It is like they are warning us:

- **The masculine critic** tells us that we are not doing enough, that we lost track of our goal, that we are lazy and procrastinators, and that we are not consistent. It is the one who says, "The project is going off track," "It is a good idea but you are not doing enough," "Go to sleep so tomorrow you can start again fresh," etc.
- **The feminine critic** says that it is not working on a deeper level, that we don't feel like continuing, that deep down we don't like the idea anymore and that we are not satisfied. It is the one that says, "What are you doing?," "Leave, it's enough," "Don't you see that it is unbearable?," "Where's the passion?"

Now some of you might be thinking: When are we supposed to listen to one or the other? If the feminine says to throw everything away and the masculine says to go to bed early to write for two hours tomorrow morning, what are we supposed to do?

They are both right, but let's see what it means to ignore one or the other:

- **If we don't listen to the masculine,** the risk is to procrastinate, to get frustrated with an unfinished project that, with the incapability of choosing which way to go once facing a crossroad on top of risking to lose sight of the goal, the meaning which translates into us becoming incoherent.
- **If we don't listen to the feminine,** the risk is that the road we are walking on with our heads down, perhaps even pushed by masculine eagerness and anger, is the

wrong road. We might end up working for months in a direction we don't like, or don't care about, or that doesn't nurture us, only to arrive exhausted at the top of a mountain and realize that it is not where we wanted to be.

Who should we listen to? The answer is both, always. But the key is to truly pay attention to what they're suggesting, so we can follow their guidance at the right moment. If we ignore the feminine telling us, "That's the wrong way," because the masculine keeps on saying, "You must paint every morning," we will end up with fifty paintings we don't give a damn about. If we follow the feminine first and find our direction, then the masculine will help us be disciplined and bring out fifty paintings we love.

In the first weeks of writing *The Creative Ambush*, my masculine allowed me to knock out about forty pages. Every morning I would set out to write for two or three hours and it was crucial to getting started. My masculine is the voice that slipped into my mouth whenever someone proposed a meeting or other commitments from 8:00 a.m. to 11:00 a.m., and the answer was: "I can't, I write during those hours." Obtuse, determined, and unapologetic. Can we meet at 10:00? No, let's make it 11:00. You really can't make it at 9:30? No, I can't make it. If I happened to sleep through my alarm and wake up late one morning, my inner masculine critic would immediately take over: "All right, smart ass, now write until noon; I don't want to hear any excuses."

The thing is, there was another voice making noise, my female critic, who had been telling me for days, "Look, this is not good. Something is missing. I don't know what but it's not good." And I pretended not to hear for at least twenty pages, writing and writing, and not listening to what the feminine was saying, to intuition. Until, one morning, the criticism was so big and violent that I didn't want to keep writing anymore. The masculine said, "Keep going, you are just making up excuses," and the feminine rebutted, "What excuses? This stuff is shit!"

So I stopped, I followed my intuition, I thought about it for two days until I saw where I was going wrong, what I didn't like. I found a new mood, so I rewrote everything and picked it up much faster than before.

The masculine is also the practical critic, the one who tells us, "You're not following the goal you set," "You said you were going to write a fantasy novel, but this is becoming something else," "This is not what the client asked for. You are not following the brief, stop and go back." He is definitely the most judicious and that is why, especially at work, we are tempted to follow him more. Meanwhile, the feminine is there shouting, "Who cares about the client! That moron! Do whatever you want! It's much better that way!"

We must choose sides once again to understand how to channel these "suggestions." If we are asked to design a logo with specific features and we go completely off target, will we be able to then support our case? There is no right and wrong: I can go to a client and say, "Look, what you asked me for didn't make sense, and I preferred to go in this other direction," and the client might even appreciate it. But what if they were to tell me to go to hell? Would I be able to make my case? We could decide not to be too extreme and find middle ground. We could make two proposals (which is usually the norm), one more masculine and the other more feminine: the first following what the client wants, the second following what we want.

Usually our masculine part is not wrong. He is rational, calculating, and judgmental: Of course he is always right. Fortunately in the creative field, being right is useless; in fact, those who want to be right at all costs are the least creative people (up yours! Ha ha). Thus, the feminine side takes on unprecedented relevance, precisely because it is the one that pushes us to go where we really want to go, even if we cannot prove that it is the right direction. The feminine part is the one that leads us toward the feeling.

For this reason, ignoring the feminine critic is dangerous. Let's look at the example par excellence: If we don't like the job we're doing, it's frustrating, it's not good for us, our feminine will be felt by an increasing strength manifesting itself on a physical level with migraines, stomach aches, gut problems, and so on. Undoubtedly, the masculine will be right—we need that job, it's a good career move, we're climbing up the ladder, it looks great on our résumé, and yada, yada, yada—however, all of those logical and great points are useless for us. Try having a nervous breakdown and then tell me how you get out of it using logic. The masculine can help us to calm down, to not rush into any decisions, to remind us that we have bills to pay and that it might be sensible to start sending job applications to other companies before we get fired. But ignoring the feminine altogether leads us toward a terrible, increasingly empty life in which we are deprived of our energy and, worst of all, we no longer recognize ourselves or even remember what we used to enjoy doing.

Lifesaving exercise

If we were to feel split in two—on one side, the feminine saying one thing, on the other side, the masculine rebutting—and we felt unsure which side to listen to, let's not stay at the crossroads for too long. This division is another way of splitting ourselves. Instead, try to jump on either side—choose randomly if you must. It is an arbitrary decision I'm talking about: "I will go right like the masculine says!" or "I will go left toward the feminine." Try it out, see what happens, and always remember that tomorrow we could go the opposite way.

For example, if the masculine says, "Keep on writing," but the feminine screams, "No, this is not good," I can choose to follow the masculine for a couple of days and see if by working hard I can fix that something that is not adding up (it could happen!); or I can stop, as the feminine suggests, so I can review the text and pick it up later on.

Likewise, if the feminine says, "Quit, this job is killing you," and the masculine retorts, "Are you serious? You get paid big bucks and you have a family," I can decide to follow the feminine for a moment; I can dream of a different life, look at job offers, and contact other companies—or I can calm down, as the masculine suggests, and focus on the financial benefits of my job. How do I feel on one side? How do I feel about the other?

PART IV

The Process

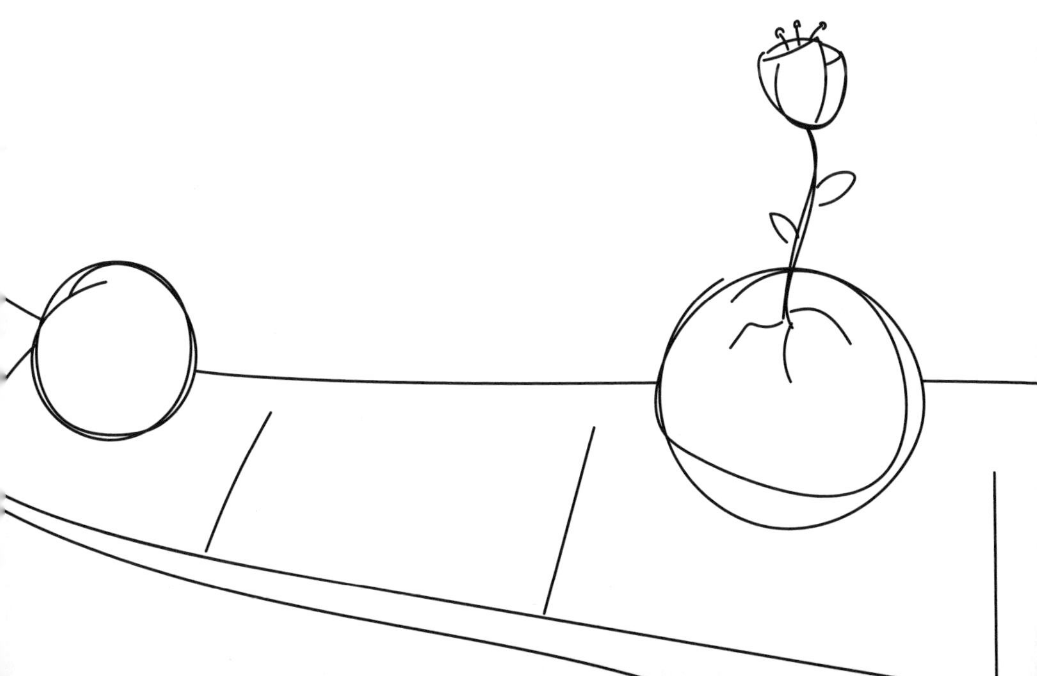

Getting down to earth

So far we have caught a glimpse of what creative living is all about, the responsibility of doing and cocreating one's own reality, of being open to something and then having the audacity to face it with action, deciding who we are and backing it up with solid facts. We have seen how to begin to chart a path to follow and how this path is not as linear as we would like but rather turns into a constant storm that we must necessarily get used to.

Before we sink further into dealing with discomfort, I thought it best to take a break, get down on the ground for a moment, and find some footholds to hold on to so that we don't fly away in the process.

I am sure that the more impatient among you must be thinking, "It's fine to define who I am; it's fine to define intuition and action, the masculine and feminine, but this is all talk. What must I actually do?"

That's a good question, to which I doubt there is a single answer. Every creative person finds their own modus operandi. What I can do is show you my personal creative process (a synthesis of all my experience) in the hope that you may be inspired to build your own.

My creative process

As I think is clear by now, the diagram on the next page is an idealization, an afterthought of a clean and perfect path. In reality, the steps are stretched out and placed in different ways; you might miss a piece, realize you've done something stupid, and have to go back. The usual. I think the advantage of having a reference process is the possibility of comparison with an "as it should be" that can help us find ourselves if we get far off track.

This is what I usually do, following this order:

1. Intuition

I let the ideas come and I gather them and observe them, as if I were a farmer walking through the orchard where apples are plentiful on the trees. I haven't picked them up yet. As I mentioned in the first chapters, I create a box of "ideas not yet to be developed" and fill it with no hurry.

2. Action

When I feel a pull toward one of the ideas, I bring it into the land of reality, taking a decisive, definite action from which I choose not to turn back: I jot down the outline of a novel; I buy books on a particular topic; I plot out the basic points in my notebook. In short, I start working on it.

3. Evaluation

I develop an awareness about the idea I am working on in terms of usefulness and risks. I ask myself, "Is this useful to anyone? Or is it something I am doing just for me?" For example, if I am working on a product for writers (like Fabula), I already know that it will be useful and that I can sell it relatively easily (because it has purpose!). If, on the other hand, I

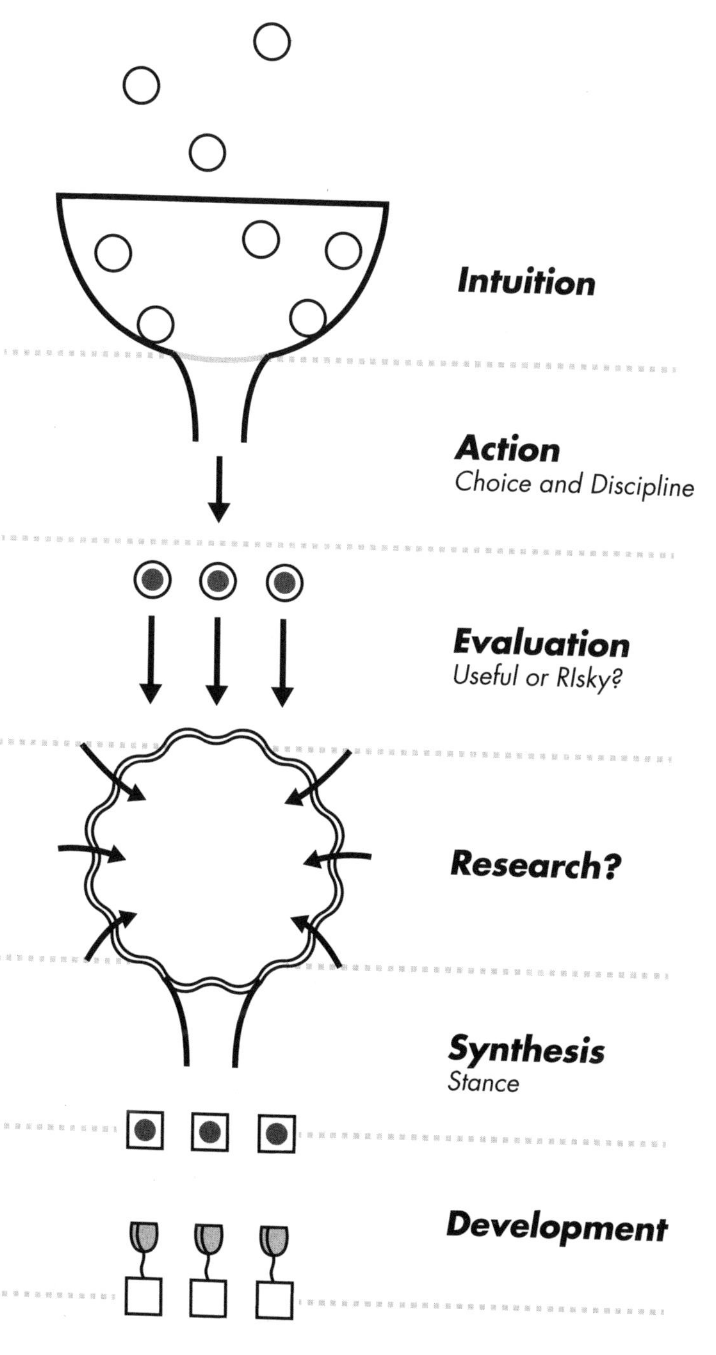
Intuition
Action
Choice and Discipline
Evaluation
Useful or RIsky?
Research?
Synthesis
Stance
Development

want to write a literary novel, there is no objective utility, so I have to be aware that the project will be much riskier. This is where the famous division between art and design, between genius and actual creation, lies. There is no right or wrong; however, it is good that I know what I am doing. Am I doing it just for me or am I hoping it will make me money?

4. Research

Do I need to study before I can work on this idea? Should I gather external elements to keep on file? This assessment is crucial. In the case of Sefirot's products, research is always a must: For Edito, I synthesized over ten self-editing manuals; for intùiti, I condensed thousands of pages written on tarot; for BAD, I studied texts on design, business, and market analysis. For this book, however, I made a diametrically opposite choice: I refused to read or take cues from any other text to avoid rehashing material from others. I wanted it to be from my own experience alone. When I am at this stage, I ask myself this very question: What do I want out of this?

5. Synthesis

At some point, you must pull the threads of the external or internal chaos. This is called *synthesis*. After reading twenty textbooks on a particular topic, what is the highest common denominator? What is the heart of the novel? What is the impact we want to have with this specific project? In short, where are we positioning our work, but also ourselves as authors, designers, and developers?

When I get to this point, I always choose a hard stance. It is a completely arbitrary choice. With Fabula, for example, we decided that we would adopt two specific narrative structures—the hero's journey and the three-act structure—over all other existing structures. With BAD, I decided that the best way to approach a project holistically would be to interpolate user, competitor, and business analyses. This entire handbook is founded on the belief that you can't really teach creativity but only inspire it.

These are all stances. The beauty of it is that there is no right or wrong because they are made up of your personalities, and your choices, so they are questionable. Someone can come to me and say, "Matteo, your book is full of nonsense and bullshit. Lateral thinking is the way to go," and I can choose to dump a glass of wine on their head. That means taking a stance! Without doing that, we are just aloof and we don't help anyone.

6. Development

When the track is laid, I can finally devote myself to developing the project. I allocate a time each day to write, plan, draw, etc. until the whole project is finished.

Application example

For Fabula Deck, the writer's tool I published with Sefirot, the process went roughly like this:

1. **Intuition.** I was editing a novel and, finding it difficult to visualize the whole structure in my head, I wrote the various passages on sticky notes and hung them on the wall. At that moment, I thought, "It would be so cool if I had a reference structure to hang on the wall as well!"
2. **Action.** I dwelled over that idea for months, then one day I bought the book *The Writers's Journey* by Vogler; I read it over a weekend and I called my best friend at the time (who would later become Sefirot's cofounder) and I said, "Let's make a tool for writers!"

3. **Evaluation.** It was not a work of art. It was a product that was meant to help people. We weren't the only ones who had to like it: It was a tool that could be sold.
4. **Research.** We read several books on narratology to make sure that what we were doing made sense. Not only that, we also tested the various structures to make sure they worked!
5. **Synthesis.** The stance here was to choose the hero's journey and the three-act structure as universal standards. This is not a choice to be taken lightly: It means that we are stating, "Whether you want to write a comedy series or *The Catcher in the Rye*, with this structure you will be able to do it."
6. **Development.** Once the structures were chosen and the content synthesized, we worked on the product itself, the graphic rendering, the drafting of the booklet, and so on.

Second application example

For *Mario*, one of the novels I wrote, the process went like this:

1. **Intuition.** I was leaving for China and I kept on seeing images in my head that haunted me, scenes from my life that seemed to want to talk to me.
2. **Action.** There was one specific image that nagged at me, and one afternoon, I decided to write it down in the form of dialogue. The next day, I continued, changing the type of narrator, and I found that exercise amusing.
3. **Evaluation.** No one would ever publish something like that: I wanted to change the narrator every chapter and

talk directly about my life, and write without knowing where I was going. I was having so much fun, though, so I decided I would continue and do it for myself.

4. **Research.** I was going to draw inspiration from my own experience. It was going to be an autobiographical novel.
5. **Synthesis.** I wanted to tell the truth, to reveal myself completely. I realized this around the sixth or seventh chapter: I wanted to lay myself bare, get naked. It wasn't just a story—what mattered to me was to seek my truth.
6. **Development.** When the synthesis was clear, I wrote the second half of the book almost on the spur of the moment.

The importance of the evaluation phase

The moment we evaluate whether the idea is useful or not serves us to understand what we are investing our energies into. Are we trying to create something useful for our current job, for our career, something that we will be able to monetize, or not? Are we embarking on a risky operation?

The risk I refer to is that of working for two years on a project for which we will not be able to find a place: a novel that is not published, a piece of work that is not sold, a project that is not made.

It is important to make this assessment not to avoid risky projects outright, but to know exactly what we are doing. If I start writing a novel thinking, "It's going to be the next *Harry Potter*, it's going to make me rich; I'm going to drop everything else and devote myself solely on this," I would be a fool. If I am working on a series of paintings portraying cats that I like, however, I stop because I think, "Maybe these are not very marketable so it is better to change strategy," I am a fool two times over.

We must be aware of what we are doing and why we are doing it, keeping in mind that a worthwhile project is not necessarily bound to be successful. It is just less risky. If I work on a new writer's tool, I am almost certain that it will be a good investment and will do my company good in financial terms as well. If I get to work on a more whimsical project that doesn't solve a real problem, well, I have to be aware that it might be a bust.

That doesn't mean I shouldn't do it! I just need to be aware of it. If I decide to take the road less traveled, I cannot do it thinking, "Ah, it will surely be paved."

Intùiti, for example, was not a useful project. When I had the intuition to create a deck of cards for creativity, I was starting from a need of my own that was so desperate and deep that I was not sure it was shared by anyone else, and even if so, I was not sure that the solution I adopted (working on myself through the use of archetypes) would be willingly accepted. It would have been much less risky to make a deck of cards for lateral thinking! Or an item like the answer book, which is simpler and easier to understand! Even knowing this, I worked for two years on intùiti and five more to find a way to communicate it effectively to the public.

And in the end, intùiti was Sefirot's best-selling product worldwide.

* *Frequently asked questions: "I use Design Thinking. How do I integrate it into this process?"*

For those who don't know what it is, Design Thinking is a five-step method that includes:

- empathize (identify with the user)
- define (identify the user's problems or needs)
- ideate (propose a solution to those problems or needs)
- prototyping (building the solution very quickly)
- test (prove whether the solution is the right one)

In case it is not the right solution, Design Thinking invites the designer to go back to one of the previous stages, devise a new solution, test it, and so on.

This is an effective, lean, and rather obvious methodology. Design Thinking tells us, "Find a problem to solve and be sure the solution is the right one." All designers use this approach, even Munari in his *Design as Art* refers to a similar process. And the reason is simple: It works! A useless product does not get used and thus it risks being a bad investment. Not to mention the horrible feeling of having left users unsatisfied.

When and if we decide to develop a useful project, the Design Thinking approach is invaluable. After I had the intuition for Fabula, I decided to implement it, I did research, etc., then in the development phase, I defined the problems I would solve for the users, and then I tested the solutions to make sure they were correct. The same thing happened for Edito, Cicero, and BAD.

The limitation of Design Thinking and all the methodologies that entrepreneurs and heartless designers like so much lies precisely in its somewhat tone-deaf effectiveness: Design Thinking would not have allowed me to develop intúiti, or write this manual or any of my novels; in short, it would not have allowed me to do anything risky.

To summarize—and, again, herein lies the importance of the evaluation phase—if we decide to move forward with an idea that must have its own usefulness, Design Thinking and similar tools are great, but if, on the other hand, we choose to be brave and embark on an adventure without a safety net and backup plans, in that case there is no map: We will be in uncharted territories, and that is the beauty of it.

Example of applying the process in the work environment

This process is fine as long as it is used on a personal project, but what to do when we are commissioned something from a client? For example, how do we apply this process if our boss were to say, "You need to make advertising campaign proposals for brand X"?

1. **Intuition.** We must open ourselves to ideas, possibly without forcing them too much. Have fun and pick up those stream-of-consciousness exercises we tried in the previous chapters.
2. **Action.** Are any of the ideas we have caught a glimpse of worth pursuing?
3. **Evaluation.** Let's look at the ideas one by one: Are they in line with the client's brief or are they off-topic, over-the-top, or otherwise? And, if so, can we take responsibility for pursuing them?
4. **Research.** Do we need additional information? Draw inspiration from competitors, call the client to see if they have customer feedback available that might be interesting for the project?

5. **Synthesis.** What ideas still hold up after gathering more information? Most importantly, what is our position regarding the brand? This is when we can decide to adopt a particular narrative or a basic message that will then be broken down into different proposals.
6. **Development.** Put together all the material necessary to present the five, six ideas that have made the cut.

When I say that this process is ideal and that in reality it will never be straightforward, it means that I will start to open myself up to ideas for half an hour in the office, then I will go out on the street; afterward I will get into an argument with a colleague, then we will have coffee, we will write down the ideas we have come up with, we will do some research, delete the previous ideas and consider what strong message to communicate, then other insights will come, and this will go on perhaps for days or weeks (depending on how much time we have at our disposal).

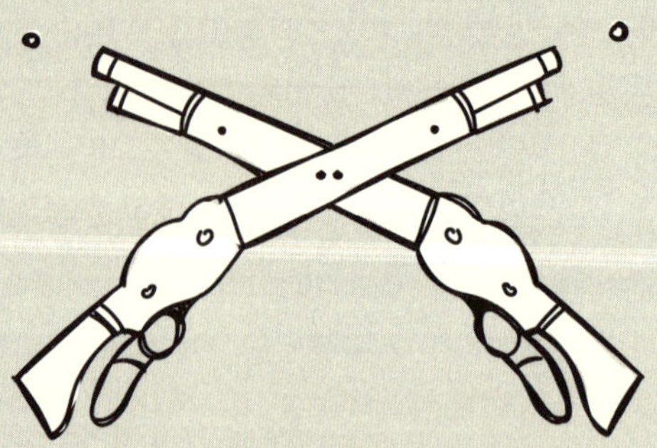

Ambush no. 5

What? Oh, you wanted a magic spell?! Ha ha. You will never amount to anything by trying to rely on the process alone. The ideal process should serve you as training, as an exercise routine to make you faster, more flexible and more attentive, then you will be thrown into the jungle with a rifle in your arms and real life will come at you with its beautiful imperfection.

If you think you can get away with the process, you are screwed and will never be creative. The sole purpose of the process is to get you back on track when you're lost: It shoots at you to remind you to drop to the ground, crawl, look around, and then get back up.

Creativity cannot be scripted.

That is the real lesson to be learned.

“Matteo, your process sounds like a pile of bullshit”

Great! Make your own! You can either take mine and tear it apart or you can create one from scratch, depending on your experiences and attitudes. My process helps me to have a frame to refer to, as I anticipated at the beginning of the chapter, I do not expect it to be universal and good for everyone.

Take a pen and paper and try to make your own; do it carefully, as if you were to teach it to other creative people at a conference. Ask yourself if it holds up. Does it work in all the cases to which you would like to apply it? And if one of your students were to raise their hand and ask, “How do I apply this to logo design?,” would you have an answer?

Stress your ideal process, find the flaws, test it so that you force yourself to deepen your whole way of conceiving and creating.

If you find something to teach others, you will have found some thing to teach yourself.

Process problems

Let's see what happens when we have issues with one of the process' steps.

1) If too much time passes between Intuition and Action

It means we never get out of the world of ideas—we don't want to get into action. We have to ask ourselves why: Why don't we like the ideas we received? Or maybe we don't believe in them? Or maybe we don't believe in ourselves? Why don't we take the first step? We can also have this problem at work, if we get lost in endless brainstorms and never define one idea; if every time one of our colleagues says, "Come on, let's get this going," we raise our hand and reply, "Wait! Wait! I just had another idea."

Let's remember that there is nothing honorable about standing still at the intuition stage. A little is fine but, as always, too much can turn out to be counterproductive. Above all, we need to know why we want to stand still. And we can no longer settle for "I don't know." We have to know and we have to face it. If we hide behind "I am scared of failure," and we say it with a veil of poetry and melancholy while sipping red wine, because we think we are cool, we need to wake up since the one thing we are not is cool. We have to face that fear of failure, to avoid becoming failures ourselves.

2) If we move too fast from Intuition to Action

Falling in love with the first idea that comes to mind and wanting to work on that is tricky business. Fundamentally, there is nothing wrong with following the very first intuition we have. In the case of Edito, for example, the first naming proposal was *Edito*. Even though we focused on the name for three weeks, we eventually went back to the first one that had convinced everyone.

However, it becomes a problem if we do this only out of arrogance. It is important to remember a basic rule: If we decide to go ahead with the first idea, it must be GENIUS. Not good, not acceptable, it must really be a bomb, stuff that makes our hearts beat fast and that, if our boss or client or Jesus Christ himself were to criticize us, we would want to defend it with our lives.

I noticed this tendency in many young creatives. In college, there is the habit of asking students to bring in one idea for a presentation and to do it with conviction, so kids end up working with the first one that comes to mind. Arrogance is not a deficit per se (I sympathize a lot with arrogant people); however, if we feel like we're the shit, then we must prove ourselves.

If you bring to me your first idea and you do it with arrogance and it doesn't make me say wow, I will tear you apart, and, I can guarantee, anyone will do the same.

3) If we are not able to do the Evaluation

Dozens and dozens of proposals arrive at Sefirot every year: people who would like to develop a Fabula for cooking, or a game to teach business management, and so on. Without judging the idea itself, often the emails they write to me are filled with phrases like: "It has incredible potential for the market!" and, when I ask them for more clarification about this potential they mention, they can't answer me, they can't tell me what problem the product solves, they haven't tested it. In short, they believe it is useful but, when cornered, they are no longer so convinced.

Another scenario is: Someone pitches a project, I tell him or her, "It's interesting. In my opinion, for it to work, it should be set up a certain way," (and I explain how), and he or she replies, "I prefer to set it up the way I decided." Great, you're taking a stance and, as you have figured out, I really appreciate it. So I say, "Let's talk again when you have everything set up so I can evaluate it." And that's when all hell breaks loose, and I get this kind of answer: "I am supposed to work on it without knowing if you're going to publish it or not? It's a lot of work you are asking for." Yes: If you want to do it your own way, there's a risk. That's what happens to all authors who share texts with publishers or work on a project for months or years, then send it in hoping to get published. That's the responsibility of the creative. At that point, they all generally vanish.

We need to be able to recognize if what we are doing is risky and how much, so that we can consciously decide whether to go for it or not. And, again, it's not an acceptable excuse to say, "But I'm not able to figure it out on my own." If you are not capable, get informed, try, do, fail, study; in short, wake up. And mind you, it's not that this excuse is unacceptable for me, it should be unacceptable for you, because otherwise you run the risk of wasting a lot of time.

4) If we have trouble with Research

At this stage, the difficulties can be of various natures: I don't feel like doing research or I don't think it's necessary; I'm not capable of doing research; I don't realize I should be doing research.

Let's start by saying this: Unless there is a definite choice (e.g., "I want to write a book about creativity based solely on my experience"), unless we are gigantic experts about that specific subject, research is always, always necessary. If we want to create an ad, we need a solid cultural background, and if we don't have it (because we are still young or because we come from another field), we need to build it. If we want to write a historical novel, we need to be experts in that specific time period, or we need to study it. If we want to create an editing tool, we have to read dozens of manuals on the subject. Simply put, we have to put meat in the grinder: no raw material, no meatballs.

With this in mind, if we feel that research is unnecessary or, worse, we don't feel like doing it, we are fools and, unfortunately, arrogant. This is the biggest problem I have encountered with junior staff: I ask them to do research and they don't do it, because they are convinced they can be more creative without outside influences. Boys and girls who have gone through three years of university think they are the shit even though, during their time in college, they have not been exposed to enough works of art, design, graphics (and not because they are stupid but because of a lack of time; I, for one, was super ignorant at the end of school). Of course, the result shows in their work. The same goes for those who want to write a novel set in Rome but have never lived there and refuse to take a trip there or read books on the subject; or those who want to write a detective story without ever having read a detective story in their lives; even those who want to make a cake without ever having read a recipe and decide to put the ingredients in by intuition. Can you see how ridiculous these statements are? Why do editors complain that there are more writers than readers in Italy? Because the manuscripts that arrive at the publishing house are often weak and denote that the author is a person who does not read. How can you write if you don't read? Exactly! How do you create if you don't do research? Yeah!

To sum it up: If we don't want to do research, we are fools. If, on the other hand, we are incapable of doing it, well, we need to learn.

Let's open Google and start searching. If I want to develop a tool for dreams, I will search for "books about dreams" and scrutinize blogs, articles, book lists, reviews, until I have selected six or seven titles. I buy them (yes, it costs money to do research!—alternatively, we can go to the library), read them, and, when I get to the end, I look at the bibliographies. These are lists of books from which that author was inspired or that are referenced in the text. Let's think of them as "pointers": Each of those six or seven books we have purchased points us to other books, which may be simple insights or real discoveries.

If we have to do graphic design research, the process is the same: I start googling, searching on Pinterest, jumping from one image to another, from one style to another, I start picking up names, "rationalism," "modernism," "Bauhaus," "Milton Glaser," and meanwhile I learn, I see, I absorb, and I build a taste.

Either way, we have to be passionate about it; it has to be a journey, a joy, a full immersion in something wonderful from which we can draw nourishment and grow. If you think, "I'm wasting my time," you are missing the point. Let's leave it then, let's do something else, but let's not play creative, because creative people, real ones, are very passionate.

5) If we have problems with Synthesis

It is like pulling the half-hidden thread of yarn that we will finally be able to unravel. This is one of the most difficult tasks, and unfortunately, it cannot be taught. One can only make an attempt. Of all the books I have read on dreams, what will be my synthesis, my stance? Of all the graphic styles, which one will inspire me for my project? It is an arbitrary choice, like deciding whether to go on vacation in Lisbon or Thailand, or vote left or right. What we need to develop is the courage to take a stance, to say, "I want to go that way." The only warning: Don't take random stances. Feel them, reflect on them, really decide which way to go. It is easy to run into people who, at the end of a search, say, "I want to go in this direction," and it is the first direction that comes to their mind, often the most comfortable one. Remember that a random stance leads to a project being haphazardly done.

And you have to ask yourself: Do you really want to throw your time away on a haphazard project?

6) If we have problems with Development

We will certainly have problems at this stage if we haven't done the previous ones correctly (if we haven't done our research or don't have a clear synthesis). If we were to have problems even after we have done research and synthesis correctly, it means that we do not have a method and/or discipline: We have all the material to write the book we want, to work on the project, to launch our business, etc., but we do not know on a practical level how to proceed.

The good news is that this is the least serious deficit: Methodologies exist and are within everyone's reach. As I said at the beginning of this book, frameworks do not help us become more creative, but they can certainly help us develop an idea. If we want to write a novel, we can learn the basics of good writing with a course, with a book or tools like Fabula Deck; if we want to launch a business or a project, we can shorten the time by studying Design Thinking,

Lean Process, Business Model Canvas, and all those other texts that are available; if we want to open a YouTube channel to talk about our passion for cats, we can learn how to edit videos and make them more dynamic and interesting.

Please note: I am not telling you that frameworks will make you an all-star, but that they will help you fill those gaps that prevent you from developing your project. If you want to write a genre novel, it doesn't necessarily mean you care about becoming a literary genius; if you want to launch your own project, it doesn't mean you want to be the best entrepreneur around; and if you want to communicate via YouTube channel you certainly don't care about becoming a professional video maker.

Let's take this step with humility and practicality: What do we need to do? What do we want to do? And how can we get it done?

7) If ideas don't arrive

I put it at the bottom even though it pertains to the first phase because if ideas don't come, the whole system goes to hell. If ideas don't come, we're fucked.

Here we can begin to really understand the importance of the feminine. If ideas don't come—or if the ideas that do come suck (which is the same)—it means that something deep inside is not working, the channel is not open, we are not open or we are misoriented. And in this case there is nothing we can do to solve the problem; we cannot shake ourselves, force ourselves, squeeze ourselves.

We can only focus on the deepest part of ourselves, to what is called inner work, which I have already mentioned, and ask ourselves what the internal problem is: What is not working for us? What is not working in general? Reaching the fundamental questions: How do we feel? Who are we? What do we want?

You can see it more clearly now: If you start with a wrong idea, which means an idea that doesn't vibrate for and with you, a half-assed idea, then you have to go through the whole process, with the risk of getting to the development stage and say, "Oh, shit, I was going in the wrong direction." And that's not fun.

So let's try to have as much respect as we can for our feminine, for that something that doesn't add up, for the intuition, for the emptiness of ideas, which can also be a very positive symptom, capable of showing us that we don't want to work on that project at all or that it would be better to set it up in a completely different way.

If we have problems at this point, let's go back to the section on page 120 and resume the exercises to train the feminine side, and do them again and again and again.

Ambush no. 6

Having a reference process makes us believe that we have a foothold, and then it unveils the tremendous truth: There is no foothold.

How easy does research and development sound now? How easy is it to be disciplined in comparison with the terrible chaos of the feminine? It is much easier to hold, to control, but in the end, it is plain and simple: Creativity happens when we let go. And it is precisely quitting that is the most shocking act, letting go of the hold on the mountain, taking a leap of faith, and falling into the void behind us. If you want to be creative, you have to have the courage to go down the most unpredictable road, the one that others might call madness, where you will no longer be in control.

If you want to be creative, you must have complete faith in uncertainty.

PART V

Faith

~~Discomfort~~

Uncertainty

This morning I paced back and forth in the living room for an hour, not knowing how to start this chapter. I wanted to talk about creative discomfort and how to navigate it, but how should I approach the topic? Should I be poetic or practical? And was it necessary to talk about it again, or was I dragging my feet? What do I have to offer, I asked myself, about this damn creative discomfort?

Something similar happened to me yesterday. I went to a Picasso exhibition and, while strolling down a corridor, my attention fell upon one of his minor works, a self-portrait made up of a multitude of compact, rapid sketches: There was a scratched, special stroke, the same one I had imagined for the cover and the vignettes of this book. I stopped and said to a friend who was with me, "That's it, that's the one! That's it!" I went home and started designing the cover, even though the book was not finished, I didn't care, and I started changing the basic color, making it white, blue, yellow, red, and sending it to friends on WhatsApp asking for opinions. In the end, I wasn't satisfied, so I thought, "Okay, it's a start"—but it didn't convince me all the way. I started asking all kinds of questions again: Am I sure that I want this to be just a book?

What if, instead, it was a book *with* a tool attached that guides people through a path made to provoke?

To summarize my situation: I am not sure how to write this chapter, how to make the cover, damn, I don't even know the nature of this product. Ha ha. That's quite a mess. That's a lot of loose ends, right? It's like hovering over a carpet of marbles. I am immersed in uncertainty, and I know that there is nothing in the world that can solve it, because there is no right choice, no wrong choice, and no one will be able to tell me, "Bravo! You found the correct solution!" In fact, there is no correct solution. There can only be the choice that I will *feel* is right, that will be right for me.

There will come a day when looking at the 216th version of the cover, I will say, "Fuck, this is it!" and I will feel it: I will have no more doubts. There will come a time when writing one word after another will feel that yes, I'm moving in the right direction, what I am saying makes sense, and it will also make sense to those who read it. It is like falling in love, like having a lightning strike, we just know it, there's no need to explain it.

Am I sure this will happen? No, no, and no! I cannot be certain, no one can be certain, that's the whole point.

I have faith that a miracle will happen. This is the hardest lesson for a creative person to learn: have faith. When real creativity appears, when we have the feeling that everything falls into place, it is real magic, and we have to find the energy to keep on going with our idea even if it feels like we are going astray, even if it is frustrating, because in our hearts, we know that at some point the night will end and dawn will come.

Finally, after two hours, I felt what was the right path for me. I went back and changed the title of this section, from "Discomfort" to "Faith," and that is what I want to convey in the next few pages: a secret to hold close to your heart, the hope of a light to follow like a beacon that will be there for you, or a star above that will know how to guide you.

Even if you feel lost, you are not lost. Even if you feel like a failure, it will not be like that forever; it is just part of the journey. When you feel lost inside a forest from which you cannot get out, you must remember that a sign will come at some point and you will see the starry sky again. Only with this unshakable faith will you have the courage to enter that forest again and again, even at the cost of losing yourself and feeling like a failure, even at the cost of being afraid and feeling uncomfortable.

The most creative people are not the most talented, nor the masters of the development stage, nor the most determined. The most creative are those who raise their hoods, tie their shoes, and smile before entering the forest.

They are the ones who have learned to love it—the forest.

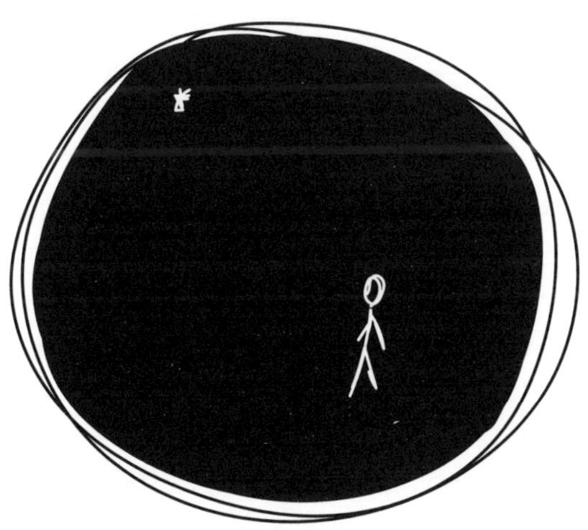

To love uncertainty: Fear of death and fear of life

Do you know why so many designers prefer UX (user experience), with its specific rules, over the more freeform world of advertising? Why do so many people want to get married? Why do they want a permanent job? Why do they buy a house? Why do they lead a life in which they are careful to limit vices, tobacco, alcohol, fatty food, etc.?

They do it to have some sort of control over something that is not controllable. We do this to forget that the only certainty in life is death. We can quit smoking and end up being run over by a car tomorrow; we can make our partners sign a contract and it will not prevent them from cheating on us; we can work for a lifetime, accumulate money with dedication, buy a house, and then be swept away by a global financial collapse. The little story of the grasshopper and the ant (whereby it is smart to be like the ant who accumulates, works, and never has any fun compared to the grasshopper who spends the summer singing) has misled us all. In real life, it may very well be that the grasshopper spends the summer singing, the ant works, and then a flood comes and they both die. Or maybe a child comes by and burns the ant with a magnifying glass. What then? Who enjoyed it more? The grasshopper or the ant?

We want to be in control to defeat this very basic truth that we all know: that uncertainty rules the world, that everything changes sooner or later, and that we will all have to die at some point. Instead of setting out for adventure, we stay in our comfort zone, where we believe nothing bad can happen to us; instead of acting on instinct, we think long and hard about every decision. In short, we fight the idea of change and death with stagnation, effectively depriving ourselves of life. Our fear of death becomes fear of life.

And this is a very uncreative attitude.

What would have happened to Neo in *The Matrix* if he had not chosen the red pill? To Alice if she had not decided to follow the White Rabbit? To Odysseus if he had chosen to stay in Ithaca with his wife? Nothing. Boring as hell. Sure, the road was full of difficulties, but this is precisely what helped them evolve and become their true selves.

With creativity it's the same story: If we decide to set sail on the seas of adventure, we will be at the mercy of a thousand and one pitfalls; if we stay within the walls of what we know, we will end up being more dead than alive. Ha ha. It's up to you.

To love uncertainty is in fact a willingness to live.

We will not take up a real gun, we will not get on a pirate ship. Our enemies will not be monsters but our arrogance, expectations, judgment, desire for fame, to be recognized, to be seen.

Our battle will be in another dimension; the darkness we will have to face lives at a further depth.

The shadow of creativity

To face the darkness inside of us, we need to ask ourselves what is scary about uncertainty. What is the real terror we have when we start writing, drawing, designing, or anything else? What is the worst thing that can happen to us when we really put ourselves out there and plunge into the world of ideas? What are we afraid of losing?

Let's try to take note of it.

I am afraid of:

- *not being enough*
- *feeling like an ass*
- *thinking, "I've wasted a lot of time"*
- *making something that is shit (so I myself must be shit)*

- *writing a decent but ultimately mediocre story*
- *being mediocre*

All these fears are the shadow of our creativity, the part of us where we try not to go, which becomes darker and darker and more hidden because we do everything we can to ignore it.

- *If I am afraid of not being enough, precisely to support my idea, I will try to be super productive, to fill my day with commitments (noncreative commitments, of course).*
- *If I am afraid of feeling like an ass, I will only do things I know how to do very well; I will avoid uncertainty at all costs in order to feel super cool.*

What happens at this point? I fill my days doing things I know how to do very well, never putting myself in a state of uncertainty so that I feel the best at what little I do, and my creative shadow, the part of me that I keep hidden and left behind, becomes darker and darker, thicker, and angrier. And, like a horror movie, a real monster takes shape: Year after year, I will no longer dare to come out into the open, because who knows what hungry beast is now hiding behind that door . . .

Integrating the shadow

There is no point in arming ourselves with a sword, flame-thrower, or whatever weapon we can find to try and set our shadow on fire. Ha ha. It is a part of us so we would only end up hurting ourselves. What we can do instead is integrate the part that terrifies us. And how do we do that? By diving into it. By embracing it.

In this case, there can be no one-size-fits-all exercise. We have to put ourselves in the position of feeling that fear, and to do that, we have to create the perfect exercise for us, a small challenge that forces us to look down into the abyss.

Some examples:

- *If I am afraid of feeling like an ass, I can turn on the music really loud and dance even if I am not good at it and maybe make some silly faces and feel embarrassed. So? Is it so terrible to be an ass?*
- *If I'm afraid I'm not enough, I can stand in front of the mirror and tell myself a hundred times, using different tones and expressions: "You're not enough. You're not enough." Who is saying that? Who does that face remind me of? And ultimately what does it mean to not be enough? Compared to what? Compared to whom?*
- *If I am afraid of writing something shitty, I can write a story and read it aloud, alone, or to a friend. It's shit, so what? Did I die because of it?*

Let's make sure we feel the way we didn't want to feel and we will find that, after the first moment of discomfort, we will say, "So what? I wrote something that is pure shit, and I felt like an asshole. Okay, I'm human."

If we want to be creative, we must be free

Free to feel human, the same as everyone else.

Because everyone, in some way or another feels that way, however long your list of fears is.

Not staying inside uncertainty, holding on to control, feeding your own shadow is inhuman. By contrast, when you can sit on your ass and say, "It's okay, it happens to me too, what's the big deal?," it is almost like having a superpower. The wisest man in the village is not afraid to put a shoe on his head and act like a fool. He is not afraid to feel stupid. He is not afraid to live.

My own shadow

The shadow is constantly changing. This year (January 2024), I went to the mountains to see my teacher and, together with other friends, we worked on the concept of shadow.

We did it through painting: We stood in front of the canvas holding oil colors and waited for the shadow to show itself.

Oil is plasticky, it never dries, so you start with brushstrokes and you can change them again and again; you can feel that the whole mixture takes a direction of its own. It's alive and it's perfect for bringing out something unconscious.

I called my shadow. I said it loud, "Show yourself, show me who you are; I'm ready to welcome you back."

And for a moment, I had a vision of a man on a high hilltop, maybe the rim of a volcano. I realized it was the shadow because I didn't like him: I was bothered by his loneliness and the barren outstretch I felt beneath him. He was the shadow because I didn't really want to see him.

I painted him as a tiny dot above the mountain in the distance, so I had the impression that a cone of energy was descending above him; finally, I wondered what he was looking at while up there all alone.

I remember my brushstrokes were angry and nervous. Was there a sea? A planet? A column of water? A door? I was putting colors on top of colors, looking for the right image, and then the wave became a fold in the universe, and there was something behind it: a fire he saw, another world waiting to be lit.

My teacher interpreted it as a sort of Prometheus looking for energy to activate a new planet or a new world. Some might say, "No big deal." Yet it is important to me.

I feel I am at a point of no return both with the company and with the way I experience creativity. If I confine to the shadows the man on the mountain, the one who dares to stand alone to enter a new world, how can I evolve? How can I find the exit to a different setting?

Seeing the shadow is also an opportunity to ask why we have rejected that part of ourselves. I embrace the madness of creativity, its aggressiveness and uncontrollability, but even I have to ask myself, "How come I put Prometheus in the shadows?" Do I have high regard for the feminine and low regard for a masculine that wants to dare? It's fine as long as the masculine is being a little soldier, writing from eight to twelve, but if he has to dare, to be the pillar of the new world, then, I don't trust him. With this work, I realized that I am very critical and ruthless with my masculine side (as my mother was with me, which was always pretty clear, ha ha).

But the crucial point remains: If I do not empower my masculine part, how can I ignite the new world I desire?

I have told you this personal experience to give you a sense of the darkness within the well, to make you want to probe the uncertainty on which a creative person must always walk while trying to keep a balance, and also to make you feel passionate about yourself and your depths.

And there is praticality in all of this, it is not just a subject for therapists to study: If I don't take back my masculine fire, how can I now renovate a company? How can I have the solidity to move to another city? How can I stay rooted, grounded, without flying away, as the world around me changes?

The nonlinear road

"This guy is talking about energies, shadows, about going here and maybe arriving there. And all I wanted to do was write a book."

Ha ha, yes, that's right. The road to creativity is not linear. You don't just walk in one door and out the other, arriving at the perfect destination. You get lost, you get immersed, you have to slip inside the maze of something more complex. The idea does not come to us because we force it or because we have committed to it and it is due to us. Maybe it comes to us because we got tired of working today and started reading a book. Maybe it comes because we went out, got drunk, and saw a bright sign, or because we took our child to school, or had a fight with our boss.

It is like love. Does anyone believe that they can fall in love on command? Or that love at first sight is something that is due? Am I going to go sit at that bar every day so after a while I must fall in love? I doubt it is going to happen. When it happens, it happens. Maybe at the supermarket, or while at dinner with friends, or even at work. It usually happens when we least expect it. That rainy evening suddenly becomes important.

If we haven't fallen in love in a while, it would be pointless and ridiculous to read a book on how to fall in love, or where to go to find a soul mate.

At best, we can try to understand why we have closed ourselves off from the world, or why we don't feel anything. Perhaps we are still hurting from a previous relationship, or we have lost faith in love, or we just want to be alone. The possibilities are endless. There is no point in looking for a formula for falling in love; it is better if we make an effort to understand why we are stuck when it comes to love.

The same should be done with creativity. Ideas, projects, and dreams come as long as we are alive and feel like falling in love with them; if they no longer come, there is something in us, a blockage, an impediment, that does not allow us to live creatively.

What if it rains love . . .

And to fall in love, you simply have to close the umbrella?

Diving in

One of the juniors I work with, Fabrizio, insists on sending me only one or two proposals for our advertisements, and I keep telling him, "Send me more." He may think I'm doing it to punish him, because I have made it a point to have at least five or six proposals per angle; however, I don't really care about quantity—I care that he dives into what he is doing.

The diving metaphor works well: What Fabrizio is doing now is sticking his head underwater for a couple of seconds and grabbing the first fish he sees. Sometimes it's a decent little fish, sometimes it's not. However, you can taste the rushed, panicked nature of the work—like someone afraid of wasting too much time. What would be better is to dive altogether, go down deep, catch a big fish, wrestle with it, bring it up, and then not settle, dive again and stand by, lurk to catch another one—the one we think is right—and keep it up until we have six, seven, eight beasts on the boat to choose from. And don't worry about how long it's going to take because, dive after dive, we will get better and better at it. Better at fishing that specific fish? No, better at withstanding the immersion.

Mind you, this is not the usual boring story about commitment or about doing your job well. It's not about ethics.

It is training in resilience.

This is the first thing I tell students when I explain what brainstorming is: "The first one you will actually take part in will make you want to run out of the room."

I remember my first experiences, I was twenty-three and I worked for a small agency in Milan. There were five or six of us, and after the first twenty minutes of spitting out ideas, we would look at each other with a half smile on our faces as if expecting the other person to be the one to add an idea to the list and take us out from the huddle of silence. After an hour, I felt like doing what Fabrizio did, throwing in the towel by saying, "All right, guys, we got a couple of ideas, so let's work on those in the meantime." Instead, the best ones would come later. We would take a cigarette break, then a coffee break, then a walk, then we would go back to the office, and, amazingly, when hours later we would reread the ideas, there were five or six decent ones that we could work on.

The other day, when I got home and started working on the cover of this book, I started pulling down dozens and dozens of sketches, so I reproduced one larger than the others, in a size that could remind me of a book, I threw it into Photoshop, and started playing with brushes to create some drafts. I did this for hours and hours. To some people, I might have looked like a fool. Did I know where I was headed? No. Did I have any idea what I was doing? Zero. I immersed myself. I had faith, an unshakable faith that something, at some point, somehow, would happen. Eventually, with proof in hand, I wrote to an art curator friend of mine to ask her if it was possible to reproduce the same thing on actual canvas, scratching cardboards placed on a rigid support such as an iron plate, tearing through the paper like in a real ambush. And that's exactly how the cover of this book was born: I put three cards, one yellow, one red, and one blue, between a 50 × 70 cm canvas and a sheet of metal, and then I attacked it with an awl.

The same thing applies to intùiti. I'm not an illustrator and I don't pretend to be one, so I'm always surprised when someone looks at the cards and says, "These are beautiful." How reckless is it to dive into a project for which, in fact, you need to illustrate seventy-eight cards? I did it: I made draft after draft of each card, and little by little, I found a style that was mine and that I felt would work. And I had faith that I wasn't wasting my time, that something was happening, that the direction was right.

Initial sketches of the cover of the Italian version of *The Creative Ambush* (pencil and pen on paper) and digital draft on computer.

On the left, cuts on cardboard and canvas on a sheet metal support. On the right, digital assembly of cuts and text.

Top left: Initial sketches of intùiti cards.

Bottom left:
Final card designs in ink.

Bottom right:
Digitized version.

Top: Display stand outlines.

Right: Printed display stand with Sole the cat.

And the same goes with every other project, even the seemingly less important ones, like the Sefirot counter display that we give to bookstores that sell our products. I had never designed a display like that, so once again, I had to dive in: I called dozens of companies and had them send me prototypes; I did tests, stacking our products in different ways, using pieces of cardboard and books, and quoting dimensions. It took me two months. I often felt like throwing everything out and setting it on fire. Then one morning, it was as if my mind had cleared—I went through the final drafts, found a solution I liked, and the display was there, ready.

Try to picture me hunched over the computer or on the table, testing and counter-testing for any project, and you will realize that, until the last moment, I have no certainty of what I will come up with. What will the new package look like? I don't know. What will the new book cover look like? Who knows. What will the color be like? No idea.

And, again, it's not so much the solution that's important but the desire to stay there and try again and again, to hold the discomfort, the uncertainty, and to have faith that, sooner or later, something will come.

Why can't we dive in?

What is so horrible about the abyss? Why are we afraid to dive? Why does Fabrizio (but I have encountered the same resistance in many other junior figures) refuse to go down into the dark and stay there? For once, he doesn't deem it necessary; he doesn't think he'll find a precious little light at some point. But what is keeping him from believing? What keeps us from writing thirty pages of a novel even to see if there is anything interesting in there? What keeps us from setting out to paint for a night even if we're only going to make a splotch of color?

If I told you that by looking at the flame of a candle in complete darkness, from dusk to dawn, without ever getting up from your chair, you could confront your demons and make a quantum leap, would you do it?

I did.

Immersing yourself in creativity is a very similar feeling. The white paper is not so different from the blackness of the abyss.

The question to ask is: "What prevents us from putting ourselves out there to such an extent?"

I will list some of the most common impediments:

1) Arrogance

One day I gave Sonia, another junior I worked with, the task of writing down one hundred possible questions to ask during an intùiti session. For example: "How can I learn how to feel?," "Why am I not creative?," "Where does my fear come from?" She arrived the following week without the questions, and when I asked her why she had not done the assignment, she said, "I didn't think it was necessary."

Her monster is arrogance; she believes she is better than everyone, and this prevents her from getting her hands dirty.

If we think we are the shit, then there is no point in diving in, because the first idea that comes to us must already be the right one.

2) The fear of being a nobody

Jeff is a product designer who has already proved himself in the field: He has a decade of experience, yet he always takes months to decide to dive in. When he hints at doing so, he never does it completely—he treats it like a game, a pastime—because he is terrified of coming up empty-handed. Never mind that he has done it before: He is so frightened by the possibility that the previous dives were just flukes that he becomes paralyzed.

His monster is the possibility of being a nobody, so it is better to put in less effort in order to have a way out: If his work is shit, he can always say, "But I didn't really try."

Often these two monsters—arrogance and fear of being a nobody—go hand in hand. We become arrogant and make little effort precisely so that we do not have to confront the possibility of feeling mediocre.

3) It is not worth it

Alessandro dreams about projects—he starts and then drops them halfway through. He is not ashamed to call himself a lazy person, a procrastinator, even worthless. If we ask him why he doesn't try harder, he replies with a slightly guilty smile and a shrug.

His monster is nihilism, the thought that nothing is worth the effort. What is the point of trying so hard? What is the point of trying to write? What is the point of struggling?

When we start thinking that the world makes no sense, we too end up losing sense.

4) The lack of heart

Susanna works for a big agency. She is a recognized professional, she takes part in brainstorms, and she pulls out ideas like candy from an always-full bag; but, if we really listen to her, we can hear that her gimmicks always have the same flavor: "We need something more vertical about the product," "We need to make a more premium proposition," "Let's try using a testimonial that embodies the brand." If we look at Susanna carefully, we discover that she is shallow, that her ideas follow a pattern, that they could fit any kind of product or service. And it looks like blood doesn't flow in her face, she doesn't have fun at work and she is always nervous.

Her monster is a lack of heart, a lack of passion.

Susanna doesn't give a damn about what she does. Somewhere in her career path, business processes have become more important than creativity, and she no longer cares about the idea that is being delivered as long as it is delivered.

Without a heart it is impossible to have faith.

When this happens to us, we can't dive in because we may find ourselves inside the depths, and once there, we might burst into tears as we say, "Everything sucks."

5) Fear of being great

Luca is a physiotherapist who would like to become a public speaker: He's been fantasizing for a while about an event during which he talks about what he knows about the human body and its problems. Unlike Susanna, he is passionate, he pours his soul into his work, and he has fun. So why doesn't he dive in?

Luca's monster is the fear of being great. He knows that if he were to start, he would be successful, and he does not feel ready. He is used to being the black sheep of the family, the one who gave up his engineering studies to do more practical work, and the idea of becoming "somebody" terrifies him. What would his role be at that point? Should he lose his eternal boyish streak?

Coming up with the biggest fish of all is a victory, and we should not forget that sometimes we are not ready to feel like winners.

6) Detachment from reality

Mary is a thirty-four-year-old woman who wants to be a screenwriter. She has a few ideas, she has tried sketching out passages of a film, but has not yet written a complete screenplay. She does research for her feature film, reads books on the subject, asks friends for opinions, even those who already work in the film industry, yet she does not dive in; she does not choose to devote an hour or two a day to what she claims has been her passion since she was nineteen.

Her monster is being disconnected from reality. What has Mary been doing until now? Why has a person who wants to be a screenwriter never committed herself to it?

If we have this monster, the immersion is painful because we have to reenter reality and confront the deadly truth: We have thrown away fifteen years of our lives doing something else.

7) Feeling miserable

Chris is a fifty-year-old doctor who works in a hospital and is a respected and well-recognized professional. His secret passion is fantasy fiction and, in recent years, he has developed a desire to write one. He has also talked about it with his wife, who urges him to carve out time in the evenings, after work, and on weekends; however, when Chris gets to his desk, a tremendous sense of hopelessness grips him and he feels miserable sitting in that small room. He stops working on the novel almost immediately.

Chris does not remember that it was his father who told him not to waste time with "impractical things," that he used to say, "In life there are solid men, and there are the ones chasing butterflies, the fools." Now, for Chris, despite his very solid job position, indulging in uncertainty is like chasing butterflies, and he feels miserable.

When we have this monster, we must necessarily strive to remember its roots. Who told us that sentence that now echoes in our heads? Who instilled in us the terror of feeling like losers if we relied on something unpredictable?

I remember, in my mid-twenties, when I called a former college professor of mine for advice because I had finally managed to get into a big agency, and yet I felt I was dying and wanted to change again, and he told me, "Matteo, be careful, because it's a short step from promising young man . . . to a loser." Ha ha.

Fortunately, I was no longer a child and his words did not break me; a month later, I quit my job. However, I had to rebel against similar sentences that I put up with my entire life.

8) Not knowing how to ask for help

Carlotta is a twenty-eight-year-old woman working as an art director in London; however, she is a pure artistic soul and would like to start developing a series of artworks. Unfortunately, every time she finds herself in front of the blank canvas, she panics. That feeling of uncertainty, of not knowing which direction to go in, deeply upsets her, as if she cannot afford to rely on anything outside of herself.

Carlotta did not have loving parents: Her mother was a drug addict and her father an alcoholic. At the age of eighteen, Carlotta left home, started working as a waitress to pay rent, won a scholarship, and, at twenty-two, moved to London. She has always done everything on her own strength, never being able to rely on anyone.

Now, when she finds herself having to rely on uncertainty, or on the universe, something comes back to her. "There's no one out there who can help me," says a voice in her head, "I have to do everything on my own," and that's why she can't dive in.

When our monster is our inability to trust, to ask for help, it becomes very difficult to trust something bigger than ourselves. If we cannot trust our parents, for example, it becomes impossible to trust even the universe (Great Mother and Great Father) and everything that does not come directly from us. In essence, we feel alone and immersing ourselves becomes almost impossible.

9) Being too much

Lawrence is a forty-year-old therapist. He has his own practice and a good career. His problem is with writing: When he is asked to write an article or essay, he fails, he gets stuck. He gets terrible anxiety and prefers to decline. For years he believed that the problem was the means—writing—that he might have some aversion to it.

Instead, Lawrence's problem is just the opposite: He has infinite respect for writing; he sees it as an almost sacred act, to which he must devote his whole self. And for him to immerse himself means to reach the most important depths of which he is capable; to surrender himself is to slip into his own craziness. "What if it's too much?" he asks himself.

When our monster is the fear of being "too much," of being over the top, excessive, out of place, we are in fact afraid of being wrong for the world. Then it becomes awful to immerse ourselves because our tendency to feel different and distant is confirmed.

10) The fear of being gaslit

Elizabeth is a thirty-two-year-old woman in charge of the dining room in a restaurant in Milan, the city where she was born and which she can no longer stand. She would like to move abroad, to go somewhere warm. She is not afraid to get her hands dirty, to start with a humble job, and she is full of drive and resourcefulness; however, as soon as she begins to imagine a new world, something stops her.

Years ago she lived in New Zealand for a long time, where she had a great time and was happy. When she returned to Italy, however, her family members did not think of her in the same way. They told her that she looked worn out, that an experience like the one she had was dishonorable, that she looked dull. Elizabeth no longer knew who to believe.

When we are unable to be certain of our reality—for example, if we allow someone from the outside to question it—it becomes difficult to immerse ourselves because we begin to be afraid of not knowing what is real. "I was fine there; however, they tell me it is not true. Either they are wrong or I am wrong." If we lose the ability to evaluate our reality, an action like the one Elizabeth would like to take (going off on an adventure), which is the very essence of immersion in a physical, not metaphorical sense, becomes a nightmare.

11) Fear of darkness

Peter suffered from anxiety and panic attacks as a boy. Although he has not had them for more than ten years, when he approaches the feeling of uncertainty, he feels as if he is falling into a black hole from which he will never be able to get out, and he runs away before falling.

When we are afraid of our dark part, it becomes very difficult to dive in, because the terror of going back into that darkness (panic attacks, depression, addiction, etc.) is paralyzing. In such cases we can learn to use creativity as a transformative process, which can help us draw inspiration from the shadows instead of shunning them and, thus, little by little, integrate them into our system.

12) Fear of wasting time

Gina is forty years old and a successful manager for a major corporation. When a publishing house asks her to write a book, she is very flattered and accepts. She organizes her own week so that she can devote ten hours to writing and calculates that in three months she should be able to finish the work. A seemingly perfect plan. However, she is unable to immerse herself; she feels as if she is wasting time in front of the page that will not fill up; her mind does not wander as it should because she halts it, almost obsessed with the predetermined number of words she should deliver each day. During each writing session, after ten minutes of stalling, Gina gives up and starts working for the company, where she knows what to do and feels she's at least not wasting her time.

The fear of wasting one's time is similar to that of those authors who say, "What's the point of setting out to write a book if I'm not sure someone will publish it?" Not knowing where to go makes one impatient; it makes us feel like slackers, worthless people. However trivial, it makes us forget that the important thing is not the destination but the journey.

Ambush no. 7

This is perhaps one of the most crippling fears because it makes one mean. Creativity and immersion in uncertainty is, first and foremost, a process concerning ourselves. By entering the forest, we discover our depths, our imaginations, our limits.

Do you think Picasso painted his works to get fame? Henry Miller wrote his books to become The Henry Miller? He became Henry Miller because he wanted to write. Bulgakov, who was blind, kept dictating pieces of *The Master and Margarita* to his wife, and certainly he didn't do it to get who knows what in return. But it also applies to great advertisers and creative people at every level: Do you really believe that an illustrator, an art director, a copywriter do what they do just for money or to win a crappy award, a piece of junk to put on an Ikea shelf? Ha ha. If they do, they are fools who will never discover their true potential.

The creative process is for you. It is a constant discovery and can only be a waste of time if you are not interested in yourself.

And, if you are not interested in yourself, you are not creative because you are no longer there: There is only the payoff, the money, the recognition, or whatever, and a cold calculation as to whether it suits you or not.

It's not that fun.

Facing your blocks

Above, I listed some of the blocks I have encountered in my creative journey. Some were (or are) my own, and some were (or are) those of friends or colleagues who attended intùiti sessions and whom I had the opportunity to learn more about because of that.

You will have realized by now that there are no rules—there cannot be in the creative field—and that every impediment is different and what we can do to overcome them also changes each time.

How do we overcome the fear of the dark? By getting into it and trying to use the dark. How do we overcome the fear of being out of our minds? By having the courage to embrace our own way of seeing the world, questioning whether we are truly lost—or if the real confusion belongs to those who fail to understand us. How do we overcome arrogance? By accepting it and seeing how ridiculous and limited we are standing on the pedestal we have built for ourselves.

The first step is certainly to see our own blocks and embrace them.

"Okay, I'm an arrogant person," "Yes, I'm scared to be out of my mind." How does it make us feel to say that out loud? Does it make us shiver, does it leave us breathless or make us laugh? Is it so terrible to admit it? So inconvenient?

Exercise

Imagine facing the blank sheet of paper. Imagine standing there waiting for something, allowing ourselves to follow whatever comes, which could be wow or it could be nothing; let's embrace the feeling of uncertainty. Will something come out? What if nothing comes out? Then what do I do?

Close your eyes and write down the sentences that your inner voice whispers in your ear.

For example:

- *"What if you're just a loser?"*
- *"Come on, you're just trying to feel important."*
- *"You're ridiculous: If you don't act, you don't exist."*
- *"You have no idea what you're doing."*

The creative discomfort we experience is fueled by these statements, which go back and forth in our heads like a relentless pendulum, leaving us overwhelmed. What can we do to confront these blocks? What battles are we fighting against these monsters?

The first step is to see where those sentences come from:

"What if you're just a loser?"
What is failure for me? Not making enough money? Not being recognized? But are these my values or those of my family? What does it mean for me? For me, losers are those who live poorly and don't do what they want to do . . .

"You're just trying to feel important."
And what's wrong with wanting to feel important? Who taught me that it is better not to dare and keep a low profile? When I announce a new project or an achievement, I often feel ashamed; I prefer to say it quietly, as if I don't want to attract the envy of others. Who taught me this attitude?

"You're ridiculous: If you don't act, you don't exist."
I identify with what I do, it's true. And it is dangerous: I risk becoming my projects, my novels. Who am I beyond what I do? Who taught me that it is convenient to have a label that defines me: art director, designer, writer, entrepreneur?

"You have no idea what you're doing."

This sounds like something that would come out of the mouth of a person who has not understood what the uncertainty of creativity is. I do know what I am doing! I am taking risks because I want to live like this. Why do I keep interiorizing ideas from people who are afraid of creativity?

If we want to face fear, the only possibility is to go in that very direction, where we are most scared to go.

I have to feel like a failure, important, ridiculous, someone who doesn't know where they are going, so I get in tune with that emotion. Do I really feel like a failure because my novel hasn't found a publisher yet? Do I really feel ashamed to talk about my successes? Do I feel ridiculous because I like what I'm doing? And do I feel silly because I write every morning even though I'm still unsure of the story's direction?

Kind of like finally walking down the dimly lit street that we used to be afraid of, just to find out that it wasn't dangerous at all.

Ambush no. 8

The point is that you have to dive in; you have to find a way to be inside the creative discomfort. I'll tell you plain and simple: There is no other way. If you can't do it, you will never be creative.

And to do that, you need to discover and overcome your monsters. Once you identify them, they can become one of the most powerful sources of inspiration. You can try it on your own or, better yet, with outside help (a therapist, a teacher, a group, some reliable friends) that pushes you a little further than where you would like to go independently.

It is not important how you do it, but you must do it. It is tiring, it is intense, and it requires energy. But if it were a piece of cake, everyone would do it. Ha ha.

Experience the discomfort

The first time I used the term "creative discomfort," I was with my friend Luca Scarcella in Los Angeles at the beginning of 2019. He is a journalist, and together we decided to do something wild: Go to California for a month under the excuse of making a documentary about the creatives who live there.

No one commissioned us to do the project. We went at our own expense; we were sick of Turin and needed new inspiration. The first week was one of pure discomfort. No one was returning our calls for interviews; we were trying to make a video where we introduced ourselves and . . . it sucked. Out of frustration, we were beginning to resent each other—we were scowling at each other. In short, we were experiencing all the difficulties of immersion, especially because we were on the other side of the world, we were spending thousands of dollars a week, and all our monsters were coming out: We were afraid of feeling like losers, like assholes, of coming back empty-handed, of feeling lonely and stupid, of not being able to produce a decent product, of throwing away a lot of money . . .

One morning, sitting on the half-pipe (in perfect California style) that stood in the courtyard of the Airbnb where we were staying, I said to Luca, "Look, let's be honest: We wanted to come to meet some people. The documentary was an excuse, right?" Luca nodded. "So why don't we keep it simple? We will shoot with cell phones, and focus on getting to know as many people as possible and try to have fun?" That's when we decided to call the documentary *Creative Discomfort*, which actually came out for the Italian newspaper *La Stampa*. The next few weeks were a lot of fun. We interviewed dozens and dozens of interesting people, spinning around LA like tops, and things started to happen: We found love, inspiration for novels, jobs, friends we are still in contact with. We even moved to Los Angeles for a while. It was, in a way, the first seed of a new world.

Going to LA to film a wacky documentary is the perfect metaphor for immersion. So absurd that it sounds like a made-up story. Whenever we indulge in creativity and uncertainty, the feeling is the same that Luca and I felt, walking the streets of LA not knowing quite where to go.

But the most important part is that this is not a story of resilience: It did not go well for us because "we hung in there" nor because "we were determined." It went well because, at some point, we surrendered, and in the middle of the street, as the California sun hardened us, we said, "Something will happen, let it happen." And it did. And that's how it always happens. You just have to get rid of all the monsters and gain some trust.

The joy of miracles

"Good Lord, Matteo, where's the faith? All you talk about is monsters, discomfort, and anxiety."

Ha ha. It's true: So far I've been talking about the difficulties we have to endure to immerse ourselves and to sustain uncertainty. But creativity is not just an ordeal; there is a prize inside the dark forest, inside the stormy sea, at the end of the darkest of wells.

At some point a miracle happens: A door opens wide and light invades the room. It may be the idea we've been waiting for; or it may be the right sentence, giving us the green light to write ten paragraphs in one sitting; it may be the perfect synthesis of a problem that had been tormenting us for days.

The word that comes to mind is justice. We feel that what has arrived might not be universally perfect, but it is perfect for us: It feels right, it fits what we were doing, and we feel like widening our eyes and jumping, turning up the music, and dancing. We become a raging river, the energy rises from our feet and goes to our heads and makes us smile. We write for hours; we design nonstop; we run back and forth for a project; we feel alive. It is pure joy, ours and ours alone, because we understand with all of our body that what has just happened is nothing short of a miracle. Something that wasn't there before is now here, and when we look at it, we wonder, "How the hell did I come up with this stuff?" and we don't care about the answer! It just happened, and that's okay, and all we can do is stand there and stare, in admiration.

That's the reward for a creative. That's why we do it, why we decide to express ourselves: to feel that point of alignment between inside and outside, between the inner and the outer, the magic of having created something that wasn't there before.

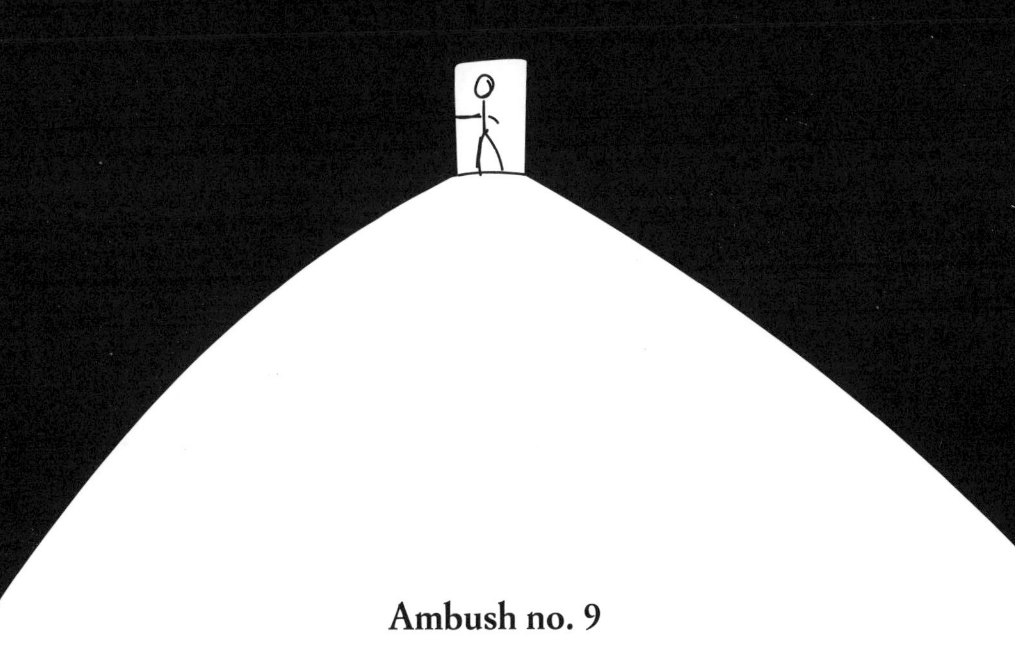

Ambush no. 9

You don't actually think you can write a masterpiece without that miracle, do you? Without that state of grace you will not create anything good, anything complete, anything successful, anything that can be acknowledged. If you deprive yourself of that joy, your life will be made of what's left: the discomfort, the nightmare.

Do you like that joy? Then you have to work on yourself, you have to be willing to see what you don't want to see, to admit what is most shameful, and trust the process.

Some approach inner work out of vocation, because they have always felt a longing for self-understanding, but most people approach it when they are desperate, when they can't stand living a certain way anymore, when they are stuck and would like to feel fulfilled.

You can also do it out of ambition. I dove into it because I wanted to be successful; I wanted to be a great writer, a great creative, and I felt that something was holding me back. It's not the best reason, I can vouch for that, but it's a start.

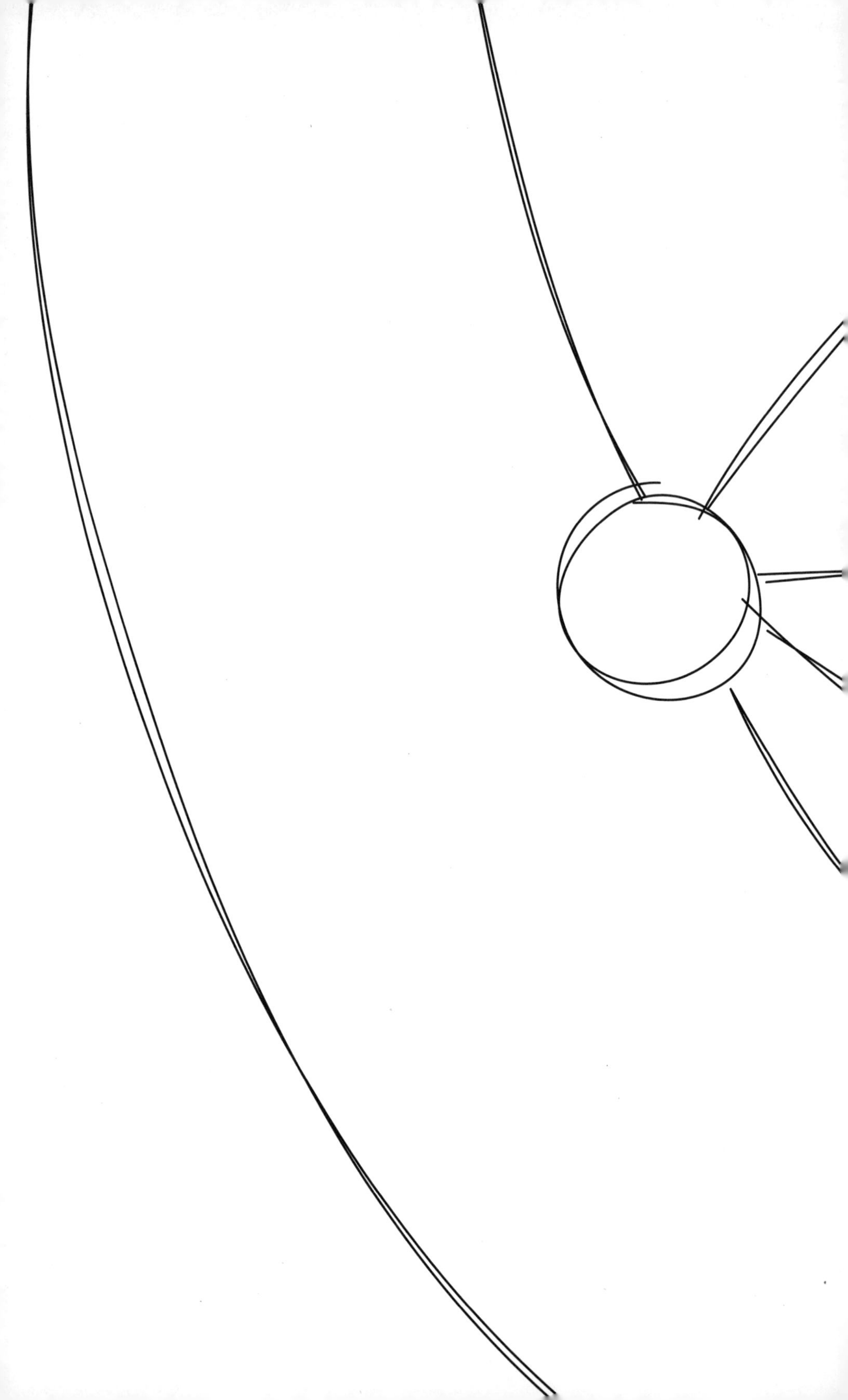

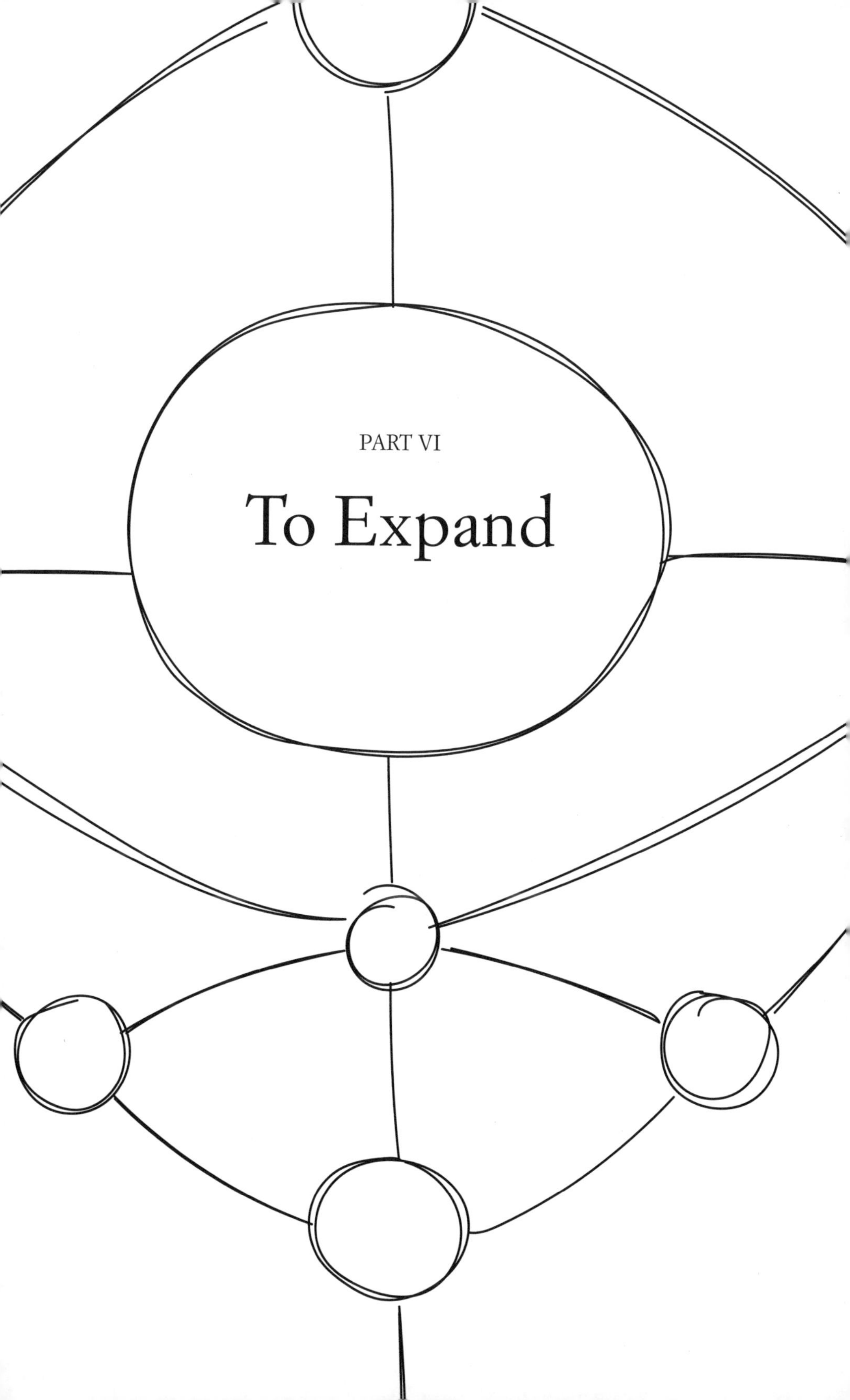

PART VI

To Expand

Us in the world

We saw how to remove external and internal blocks, how to self-structure, how to follow a process, and how to have the courage to stay in uncertainty.

Now we need to move on to the last stage: connecting internal and external, and expanding into the world.

On the ideal level, creative expansion should be a natural and necessary action: A creative person should feel like being creative; a writer should feel like writing; a cook should feel like cooking; a painter should feel like painting. Our nature should propagate into the world, like a drop falling on the surface of the water and generating a ripple. A writer who loves detective stories will write about murders; a chef who wants to feel independent will open their own restaurant; a painter who wants to explore the theme of death will paint about that; an advertising executive who wants to work at the highest level will win award after award.

Yet it doesn't really work that way. We are the sum of many aspects—who we want to be, how we feel, what we want to achieve, what we know how to do—and the wholeness that comes out of this is never a perfect sphere bursting effortlessly through a frictionless surface.

It doesn't take much for that expansion to turn into an unhappy one: A writer who loves mystery novels but stubbornly sticks to working in an office will implode; a cook who wants to feel independent but lacks the courage to open their own restaurant will have a breakdown; a painter who wants to explore the theme of death but decides only to work on commissioned paintings will end up making all of their works too gloomy; an advertising executive who wants to work at the highest level but is terrified of success will be frustrated working inside a bad agency.

To expand into the world is to be mature and aware of ourselves and what we want to achieve. Making it so the process is as it should be, natural and spontaneous, is one of the most challenging tasks we have as creatives.

This is the part of the book that I honestly find the most challenging to write, because even fifteen years after my first creative experience, I struggle with it, and I think that, on and off, everybody does. Even great writers who, for a time, feel aligned with who they want to be, after writing a masterpiece, can fall into depression; or the entrepreneur who launches a successful company and then, five years later, hates it. If we think of life as a creative work, that uncertainty we have talked about so much will always be there as a wave to be surfed, with ups and downs, depending on the seasons and eras. Who we want to be today is different from who we'll want to be tomorrow and who we wanted to be yesterday. Our expansion is constantly evolving.

We are free—that's the cool thing—free to be who we want to be and do what we want to do. But this freedom is also a great agony because, in the end, it is up to us; we are responsible for our own joy and satisfaction.

I ask myself every day whether I am aligned with what I really want to do or whether I am just bullshitting myself. I stay alert—I check in with myself—to avoid realizing one day, two, three, four years from now, that I wasted a ton of time chasing something I never even wanted. As long as I worked for others and was dissatisfied, it was simple: just quit. Since I have been self-employed and doing only what I want (at least that's what I tell myself . . . but is it actually true?), the situation seems more complex to me. Then again, I cannot fire myself.

Those questions I brought to you in Part III—Who am I? What do I want? What impact do I have in the world?—that define our expansion into this reality, those are the questions I think about every morning.

I question my true nature, what I want, and then I compare it with the way I am living, looking for alignments or discrepancies.

So many people say to me, "Wow, your job is so creative! You made it!," because they think of the tools we develop with Sefirot and associate them with a high expression of creativity. But that's not the creative expansion. It's not that I'm creative because I have a creative business, while someone who has opened an accounting firm or a restaurant is less creative.

The creative expansion is in the way I live, in the constant desire to recalibrate myself over time and to have the courage to see the truth, however uncomfortable it might be.

When I was twenty-seven, I wanted to be a writer. So after years of complaining, I finally quit my job at the ad agency and locked myself in my house for three months to finish my novel. Brave, wasn't it? Yeah, sure, for three months. When I found myself with the finished manuscript, I didn't know what to do: The truth is that at that moment I didn't feel like living the writer's life, sending my book to publishers and waiting while I tried to write another one. I felt like a loser, like Jack London but shittier. So I went back to work: I went to China to experience working in a big company, then I came back and went on dozens of job interviews only to turn down all the positions they offered me. I had to admit another truth: I had no desire to work for anyone. So I went freelance; meanwhile, I opened an online UX design academy. Things were working well but I was not satisfied. I was doing everything with my left hand, in a lazy way. Truth is I was angry and felt like a failure. At that time, I had already launched the first three products—intùiti, Fabula, and Cicero—which I cared a lot about, but friends and relatives looked at them as a hobby, the wacky projects of a moron, of the village idiot, worthless toys that no publishing house wanted to publish. And I wanted revenge: I wanted to show everybody that they were wrong, that the tools were useful and had a market, and that I was not a moron, I was right.

For that very reason, the first two years of Sefirot were happy and exhilarating. As I reached my goal, when I sold millions of units and proved myself, I felt lost because I was working like crazy to grow the company, especially to sell our products, but I didn't care about it that much. "I want to write," I repeated to myself, "what's the point of all this, if in the end I just want to write?"

I restructured the company, making it so that I could write every morning while limiting my role in Sefirot to afternoons and evenings. I wrote four novels in the last year and a half, two of them in the hands of my literary agent who is trying to place them in the very lethargic Italian publishing world.

What's next? Should I lock myself up at home like a robot and spit out book after book? "Is that all there is to me?" I asked myself.

Another truth: I need Sefirot. Without this company, all my tools would be on top of a shelf in my house gathering dust and I would feel like shit; and it is the only work I like to do (for now) that allows me to write in the morning and unleash my creativity.

So what should I have done? Design a new product? No! I really needed to challenge myself with creativity. And what better way than to write this manual? Ha ha.

So here I am.

This is the only system I know: having the courage to see your own nature and expand. Day after day. And do it again and again. All over again, if necessary. Difficult? Sometimes. Painful? Also. Exciting? Always.

Let's see how we can do it together.

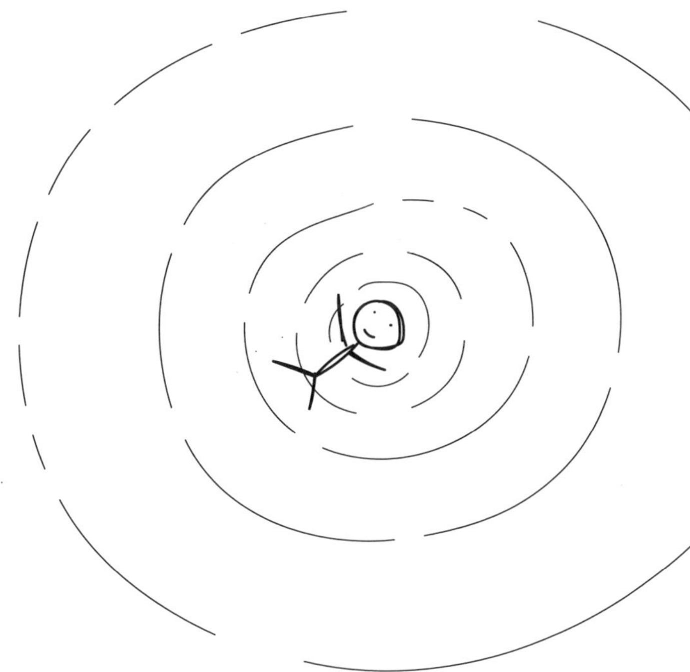

Goals and identity

Let's go back to the variables I introduced in Part III: "Who I am" and "What I want," which really mean who I feel I am and what I believe my longing (my highest goal) is.

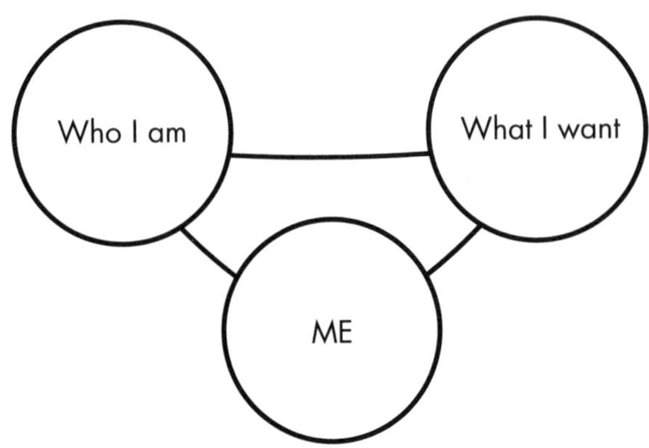

To these we can add the relationship with reality, so, "What we are doing" (who we are in a practical sense), and our "practical goal" (what we are trying to achieve in our everyday life).

To recap:

- "Who am I?"
- "What do I want?" (high goal)
- "What am I doing?"
- "What is my goal?" (practical goal)

If, for example, we are actors who have dreams of acting inside a Hollywood movie, however, right now we are working as waiters with the prospect of becoming restaurant managers, we will write:

- *Who I am: "I am an actor."*
- *High goal: "I want to star in Hollywood movies."*
- *What I am doing: "Waiting tables."*
- *Practical goal: "To become a manager."*

We will almost always find a difference between who we would like to be and our high goal, compared to what we do in reality and the practical goals we pursue every day.

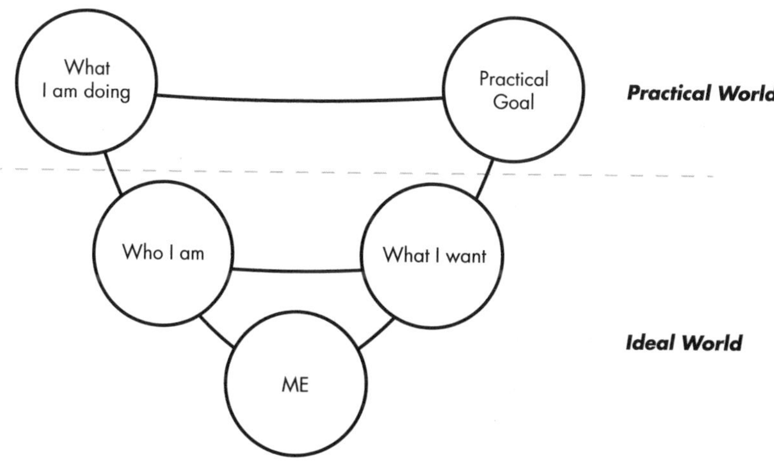

We may feel like writers and we want to be famous, but in fact, we work as advertisers while trying to step up the ladder; we may feel like chefs and want to be independent, but in fact, we work in a restaurant while we try to establish financial security for ourselves; we may feel like illustrators and want to publish our first children's book, but in fact, we work as teachers while we try to buy a house.

In short, we can feel one thing but do another, and we can dream of one goal but then be engaged in quite another. There is nothing wrong with that; however, it is necessary to be aware of it.

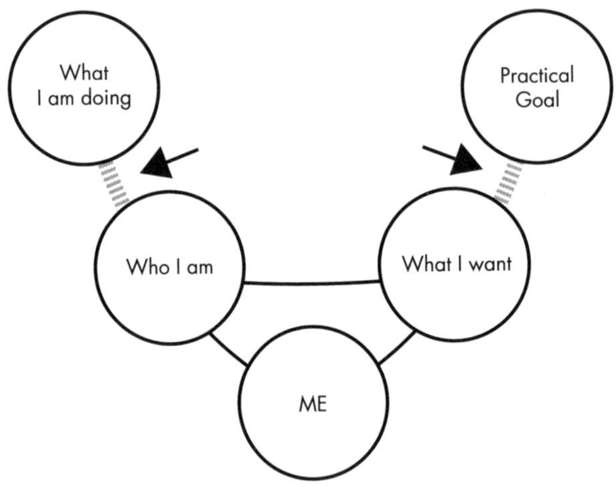

We need to assess how high and practical goals are misaligned, so we can see how misaligned we are: who we are (or who we want to be) versus how we are behaving.

We may find that we have both misaligned identities and goals, or aligned identities but confused goals, or vice versa.

Aligned identities but misaligned goals

Alex is a writer who has published several novels and now lives off the royalties from his old books while holding classes at three different writing schools. His books have never sold much: just enough to be accepted in the literary environment, yet not enough to make him a household name.

He would like to be recognized as a great writer (high goal); however, he cannot find the time to devote to what could be his great masterpiece. He is worried about money, so he puts a lot of effort into teaching and writing books that his agent offers him (practical goal).

Alex is expanding into the world in a way that is wrong for him: He is expanding as a writer (aligned identities), but as one who writes to make money, when he would like to write to express something deeper (misaligned goals).

Misaligned goals and identity

Heather feels like an illustrator and would like to finish the children's storybook she has been working on for three years now, pitch it to a publishing house, and build a career on that (high goal). But her reality is quite different—Heather is a senior art director in an advertising agency, oversees two teams, and is highly valued in her workplace. She often works long hours, so her fiancé complains that they never spend time together since, on top of everything, she has been trying to win a Cannes Lion for years (practical goal).

In summary: Heather would like to be an illustrator but she works as an art director (misaligned identity); in addition, not only does she not behave according to the person she would like to be, but she also stubbornly overcommits herself to a practical goal that does not match what she really wants (misaligned goals).

Aligned goals but misaligned identities

Carlo feels that he is a filmmaker and wants to make a name for himself in the film industry (high goal); however, he is not working as a filmmaker but as a screenwriter, and he is striving to become famous in that field (practical goal).

The goals make sense with each other; they tend toward the same direction (aligned goals).

The only problem is the kind of life Carlo is leading: He lives as a screenwriter and not as a director (misaligned identities).

Ambush no. 10

To expand in a meaningful way you need to be present in reality, which means to see reality for what it is and not for what you are telling yourself. It means looking at the current situation, understanding it, and accepting it. It is not enough to say, "I want to be an artist," if in fact your life is that of an accountant and you have not touched brushes and colors for twelve years.

If you don't recognize this, you are out of touch with reality—like those who are convinced they are living one life when, in truth, they are living an entirely different one.

Misalignments analysis

All misalignments are not the same; you have to look at them carefully.

It's not enough to say, "Oh, okay, I'm misaligned," and the trick is done. We need to dig deeper. What kind of misalignment am I dealing with? Why do I have it? What is my advantage in living this way? We may realize that a particular misalignment is not serious, especially if it is conscious and functional, or maybe that it's not even there (we convince ourselves of a lot of bullshit, ha ha).

Functional misalignment. Marco is a screenwriter who wants to have a career in film (high goal), but he works as a clerk in a supermarket to pay the bills (practical goal).

If we need the practical goal for living, for rent, for studying, while we expand at night and on weekends to reach our high goal, that's very good: The practical goal becomes functional to the high goal.

Irrelevant misalignment. Clare feels she is a writer and her high goal is to be free and independent. She ran away from home two years ago and moved to the Netherlands where she lives off of odd jobs. She will write a book someday, she is sure of it, but for now she feels free and happy. At this time in her life, Clare does not care what she is doing as long as she can achieve her high goal.

If the practical goal has nothing to do with the high goal but is not conflicting either, it may be okay temporarily. For example, if at this time we need to become financially independent and move out on our own, let's not be too hard on ourselves: What we do on a practical level is not that important compared to the joy of finally being free, right?

False misalignment. Carlotta complains because she feels she is a failed musician; she would like to be free (high goal); instead, she works as a journalist for a newspaper that has hired her on a temporary contract, and she tries her best to be well accepted by her bosses (practical goal). Carlotta does not admit it, but in truth, she does not want to be free—her high goal is a sham; she desires security and is willing to do anything to get it.

She could work in the musical field—she would gladly do so—but only if she could get a stable contract. If we convince ourselves that we have a goal but is not true, we risk feeling misaligned for the wrong reason.

Do we really want to be free, independent, great, etc.? Or is what we want something totally different?

Utilitarian misalignment. Marco feels like a novelist and would like to be famous (high goal), so he decides to open a YouTube channel to become an influencer and create a community (practical goal). He knows very well that he is misaligned and that he has to work in a completely different direction from what he wants; however, it is part of his strategy. He is convinced that if he were to achieve the practical goal (create a large community), a publisher would finally publish his book.

This is the most dangerous of all misalignments because it is consciously mean-spirited: Instead of investing our energies toward our dream, we choose to take an alternative path believing we are smart. We do Y to achieve X. I fell for it once, too: "If Penguin would publish Fabula," I said, "then someone would publish my novel." What nonsense: If we become influencers who talk about politics, then they will ask us to publish a book on that topic, certainly not a novel.

Sometimes we can be aligned, yet something can still be wrong:

"Wrong" goal. Becca studied design and started working as an advertising designer, which was her dream. Unfortunately, she had a terrible time at an agency in Milan. She was mistreated by her boss, and even at home she was struggling because her parents did not fail to constantly remind her that "it would have been better if you had studied engineering instead of that nonsense." So she moved to London where she now earns 6,000 dollars a month. Her goal is to succeed in order to rub it in her parents' and former colleagues' faces. Becca is about to move to Hong Kong, where she will be given leadership of an entire division and a staggering pay raise. She is perfectly aligned, but she is not happy, because the goal is not really her own: It comes from revenge and sooner or later she will have to face it. When we have the wrong goal, one that does not really reflect our nature, in the long run, we risk living someone else's life.

In Becca's case—which was also my case during the first two years with Sefirot—it can be helpful to become aware that revenge was only one part of her life, and now that she is finally free of it, she can acknowledge her own more authentic goals.

A goal imposed by someone else. Emma always wanted to be a lawyer and gain financial stability (a high goal), and now that she is working in a renowned firm and has achieved her goal, she wonders if that was really her desire. She gradually realizes that it was her parents' words, "There is nothing more important than a stable job and a home," that led her toward that goal.

The important thing is to realize this as soon as possible. Again: Welcome, Emma, to a new stage of your life!

Lack of goal. John has a company with three partners. They make skin care products and they are trying to make the business work (practical goal); however, he has no idea what he really wants or how he wants to feel. He has no high goal to achieve and he feels lost, like a leaf in the wind.

When this happens, the problem is serious and deep. If we can't identify a goal and feel lost, it means we can't even feel when something makes us feel alive—we don't know where to look. We need to recover the inner child, that part of us that wants to live, feel, and understand why we have lost it.

The key to everything: truth

How do we see where the misalignments are, the lies we are telling ourselves and our limitations?

By telling ourselves the truth, by having the courage to see it and get hit by it.

When I quit the agency to finally get into writing, it was "easy" to see the truth, because I had been complaining for years about work and not being able to devote myself fully to writing. But the next step proved more punishing: admitting that the writer's life (as I experienced it at the time, at least) did not appeal to me. That truth left me soft-legged. "I don't want to work in the agency," I said to myself, "and I don't want to live a writer's life. Oh god, then what the heck do I want to do?" It was terrible to learn but, if I hadn't admitted that, I wouldn't have opened Sefirot three years later.

Let's look at what we wrote:

- *Who I am: "A writer."*
- *What I want: "To be recognized as a writer."*

We must ask ourselves: Is it true? How come we say we want to do that and then we do something else entirely? Are we sure that's really what we want?

It is uncomfortable, very uncomfortable, but we have to go there, every week, every day. Is it possible that we say we want to write and then we never write? How come we say we want to act but can't find the time to do it? Isn't there something out of balance? Either we are cowards, or—and that can happen too—we have set our minds on the idea of being writers, actors, designers, etc., when instead we want to do something else. Maybe we want to be restaurant managers, maybe we like that better but won't admit it; maybe we want to break our backs in the agency to win in Cannes, maybe right now we need that kind of recognition.

"But how do we know what the truth is?"

There is no question when it comes to passion. It is always a big fat yes. A writer feels like writing. An actor feels like acting. A chef wants to cook. A designer wants to design. If this urge is not there, if it has to be forced, if we feel too tired to devote ourselves to what we say is our passion, something is wrong.

It's easy: If you feel like doing it (and you actually do it!), it's a passion; if you don't feel like it, it's not.

It's the same feeling of enjoyment we get when we are done at work and can't wait to go play tennis, or PlayStation, or read a book that is wooing us, or make love to our partner.

We are pulled to that action as if by an irresistible cord.

In late 2011, I spent four months in Alessandria, my hometown, between the end of college and the beginning of my first job. My friends and I started playing bridge and we wanted to play every free moment we had, it was an obsession. We played in the evenings until two in the morning, on weekends, we would never stop if not for meals.

At that same time, I was drawing intùiti cards, and every morning, I would wake up and look forward to going to the library to dive in. The feeling, minus the excitement of the game and the complicity with friends, was very similar.

It happened again the following year, in Amsterdam, during what was unexpectedly one of the happiest months of my life, when we were working day and night on the launch of a startup.

When things go as they should, we feel vibrant, alive. We feel like writing, designing, painting, drawing, thinking about our dream, working on it. It feeds and fulfills us, regardless of the outcome.

That doesn't mean it's senseless joy all the time. During the month I spent in Amsterdam, I was not always happy, just as I was not happy designing intùiti. We can be frustrated while playing PlayStation because we would like to win but we can't; similarly we can be frustrated because we can't get on with the novel, or because the cover of the book we are designing doesn't convince us. The point is that we vibrate and feel passionate, for better or worse.

If, on the other hand, we don't feel vibrant, in the long run we die out, like a plant deprived of light. And, the longer we pretend nothing is happening, the longer it will take us to recover.

Ambush no. 11

Do you feel vibrant? That doesn't mean happy and carefree. Do you feel alive? Electric? Do you feel like getting up in the morning and doing what you do? Or do you feel that you are shutting down?

Because, if you keep chasing that goal that serves no purpose or, even worse, if you keep telling yourself that you have a passion but then you miss it because you don't do anything to go in that direction, you will get sick.

It is better to admit that you don't have that passion, that your job sucks and you're only in it for the money, that you don't know what to do and where to look, that you've taken too many decisions lightly (so far). Give yourself a good slap in the face so that the castle comes crashing down and it leaves room for something new.

The whole truth lies here, in listening to yourselves and having the courage to laugh about it.

The real goal

In the end, the real goal is to feel alive. Which in my experience means aligning as much as possible what we really want with what we are doing. Only if we feel alive—for better or worse—are we truly creative.

As I mentioned at the beginning of the chapter, feeling alive should be our natural condition—it's just a matter of being able to return to it.

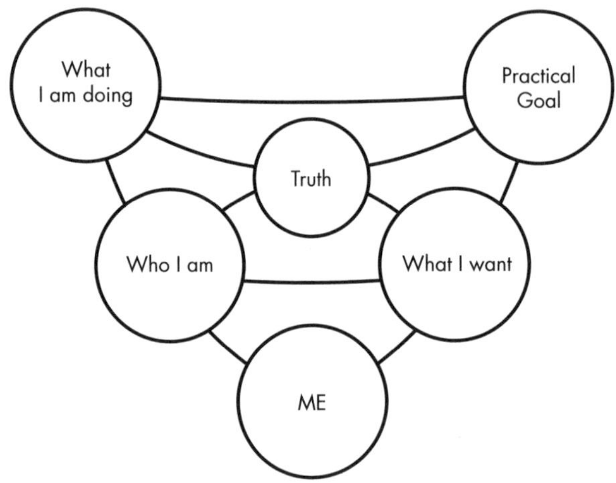

True nature overflows

If we allow ourselves to feel, our true nature gradually comes back. Just watch for the signs.

When I worked at the agency in Milan, I liked the work itself; however, the hours and the location killed me. I wanted to go brainstorming in the park, and I wanted to work when I wanted to work, but there was so much downtime! The downtime killed me! The thought of having to sit in the office while browsing Facebook because I had no assignments that afternoon distressed me like nothing else.

My nature is free-spirited. And as much as I told myself, "But there's a schedule to keep," inside I wanted to scream and run away. It would take me eight years to accept that I could not work as an employee.

At seven I bought my first deck of tarot cards, at eight I started programming websites, and at twelve I wrote my first novel. These three passions—cards, the digital world, and writing—haunted me in every job, in every country, until I could find a system to put them all together.

Sometimes it is others who see the signs and tell us.

When I was twenty-three, my teacher told me, "You can't work for someone else. Freelancing, is better for you." And I refused to listen. I thought, "Fuck that! I don't know how to get clients; I want to work for famous agencies."

Then when I was in the big agency, one of my colleagues took me out to lunch to tell me, "It is clear as the sky that this kind of work is not enough for you. Anyone can see that you want to do more." And I thought, "Can everyone please leave me the fuck alone?"

They were right: They saw the signs of my true nature, which from time to time would overflow, peep out, show itself.

We must learn to unearth these clues, to give them importance, both the positive and the seemingly negative ones. If we are talkative and like to be the center of attention, we might be happier taking space, either on a stage or in front of a camera. If we are lone wolves and don't like to work with others, it might be better for us to work as independent consultants.

Let's ask ourselves:

- What is my true nature?
- What are the breadcrumbs that my true nature has been leaving for me to follow?

"Is it a good idea to follow our true nature?"

Albert, a friend of mine, was studying to be a doctor but it was not in his nature. The only thing he was really passionate about was poker. He didn't think about anything else. He didn't care about college and spent every free evening at the poker club, playing Texas Hold 'em. His parents, girlfriend, and friends convinced him that he was a loser: "You'll never amount to anything" was the sentence they used to say to him, in different forms. What was amazing about Albert was that, while he could not remember a single notion of medicine, he knew everything about poker playing strategies. After a while of attending the club, he was asked to work there in the evenings as a croupier. Eventually, Albert found the courage to drop out of college and go to Sicily to take a three-month course to work in casinos. After two years, he was in London and earning more than a doctor.

Am I saying that if you follow your dreams you can make it? No, what I'm saying is that if you feel alive while doing what is in your nature, then you have the energy to excel and the world responds accordingly.

Another friend of mine, Daniele, has always had a gambling habit. Cards, slot machines, betting. He burned entire paychecks that way, and when he realized that it was not so much the thrill of loss itself as much as the card game that excited him, he turned to bridge, a passion that within two years showed Daniele's true nature as a professional player. A guy who had never been interested in studying was now staying up late, reading books deep into the night. When the time came to make a choice—the secure job he had or a career playing cards—he chose the first option. I don't think he is too happy, and I hope his nature will come calling soon.

Contrary to what frightened parents teach us about our future, our true nature is the best way to achieve prosperity (a good income), because the energy we show when we feel alive is a resource that has no equal.

I have never had so much success, in terms of recognition and financial return, as with Sefirot. The company worked because the amount of energy I threw in it was like a tsunami: I never stopped, I always had ideas, always wanted to do and grow, I felt in my place, and most of all I loved it! And because of that, I was never tired.

If your true nature is to be a photographer, you can't think that you would make more money working as a clerk (a job you hate) than you would make taking pictures with your energy running high. The same goes for an engineer who wants to be a pizza maker, for a teacher who wants to be an osteopath, for an entrepreneur who wants to be a sculptor.

It is in the awakening of your nature that you can really make money, because you will be expressing an energy you have never seen before, and money is nothing but energy of a different kind coming back to you.

"What if I feel like an amateur?"

Sure, I'm awakening to my nature as an artist and it's been ten years since I picked up a paintbrush. Or my nature as a farmer but I don't even know how to plant a zucchini.

It's normal to feel like an amateur and think, "I should have done this earlier, now it's too late."

There are people who learn at twenty and excel at twenty-five. What prevents you from starting to learn at thirty-five, forty, and then excelling at forty-five? Better late than never, don't you think?

Do you have any idea of the amount of things we can learn and the mastery we can achieve in a couple of years when we really enjoy something?

Enhancing your true nature

In 2019, Sefirot's marketing manager gave me a heads-up to start writing a newsletter with which to keep in touch with our customers (and to use as a selling tool, of course). For months I refused: The idea of writing every week a series of petty gimmicks or uninteresting tips, basically the whole concept of doing a newsletter, made me nauseous. Yet I knew the marketing manager was right about one thing above all: It was stupid not to keep a relationship with customers.

At some point I said to myself, "Okay, I have to do it, but how can I do it staying true to my nature?" I am a writer, a creative, and I want to strive for authenticity. How do I use that to create a newsletter that I feel like writing every week?

That's how the Creative Bulletin was born, a weekly email in which, for the past four years, I have been narrating what's really going on inside the publishing house, our joys and sorrows, without neglecting even the uncomfortable and controversial episodes (a habit that several times has earned me response emails filled with insults). Over time it has become almost a product in itself, so much so that often, when I meet someone at fairs who knows us, one of the most recurring things I hear is: "Don't stop writing the bulletin, I love it."

The bulletin works because I love writing it, which has allowed me to be consistent for over two hundred releases; and I am convinced that the joy and passion that drives me can be felt and that is precisely why the readers like it so much.

With the newsletter, I have enhanced my nature. I made a newsletter that allowed me to express myself. The same thing happens if I have to write content about creativity: I could start a blog, or become an influencer on Instagram. But it's not in my nature—I don't like blogs or reels—I would quit after a month and struggle terribly. Instead, I like to write books, so I write a book.

When we identify our nature, it becomes much easier and, yes, even more productive, to follow it and enhance it.

Let's ask ourselves:

- When was the last time I did something in a way that was in line with my nature?
- How can I do everything in a way that is in line with my nature?
- How can I use every opportunity to be me?

If we want to become TV series directors and we are working to produce Facebook commercials, why don't we come up with an ad that looks like a sitcom? If we want to become editors and we are working for a leather company, why don't we propose to edit their blog or a company magazine? If we want to become entrepreneurs, why don't we suggest to our boss to give us a task in which we do new business and look for new clients and sources of income?

In short, once we have a better understanding of who we are right now and what we want, we can move in that direction. And rest assured, no boss or client will ever turn their nose up at our proactiveness.

If an employee of mine with a passion for board games said to me, "Matteo, next week I'd like to pitch some educational games for Sefirot, and if you like them, I'd like to be the one to work on them," I'd be over the moon. I would have a more motivated employee who really wants to express themselves in what they do. I can't ask for more.

Recognition

For years I would have wanted someone important—like a literary critic or the editor of a major publishing house, even an outstanding professional—to recognize me as a writer. I would have wanted them to read one of my novels and then say, "Matteo, you are a good writer."

I needed to feel seen, to know that I was not just a fool, a little kid pretending to be a writer.

We all have that need. And the more we feel proud of what we do, the more the terror of being out of touch with reality grows, and consequently, the need for someone to tell us, "You're not delusional," grows as well.

The great paradox of recognition is that if it is only external, it is never enough. Like when someone reassures us that we look good in a shirt or a haircut, but we feel ugly. Recognition must come from within. Think about it: If we are unable to see it ourselves, who could ever convince us?

The day I chose to see myself was the day I decided to publish my novel *Mario* with Sefirot. I announced it to our community with the newsletter, and I stayed up until three in the morning writing what turned out to be the most difficult email of my life. I was shaking with shame: I felt like a fraud, a clown, because I was self-publishing. Who did I think I was? How could I recognize myself? Finally I said to myself, "Knock it off. If you don't believe you're a writer, who could possibly believe it?"

When, four months later, a critic wrote a good review of *Mario* in *Robinson*, the most important literary insert in Italy that comes out with the newspaper *La Repubblica*, I realized that . . . I didn't need it anymore. Ha ha. I was happy, over the moon, excited, but it was no longer a necessity, because I had already recognized myself. And in that moment it was crystal clear: If I didn't recognize myself, I would never have been satisfied with that review; I would have wanted another, and then another, and another. My thirst would have never been quenched.

We must have the audacity to recognize ourselves; otherwise, it becomes impossible to really enter the world. If I hadn't dared to create a site for my products and say, "Here they are, buy them," no one would have ever bought them or thanked me for creating them.

There is always a moment of dread, it's like knocking on the door of the boss or an important person to announce, "Hey, I'm here, I exist, and I think I have something good to give."

It is not arrogance: It is an additional sense of reality, one in which we begin to become aware of our value and potential.

We become aware of it because we are proud of who we are and what we are doing.

Let's ask ourselves:

- What is recognition for me?
- What needs to happen for me to feel recognized?
- Why can't I recognize myself?

Pride and mediocrity

During my classes, juniors and students often submit pitches that are not great. I look at them for a few seconds then ask, "Do you like them?" They usually hesitate then shake their heads no. So I ask, "Why did you bring them to me if you don't like them? What did you expect?" Maybe a pat on the back, I wonder. Maybe they want me to tell them they're okay? Maybe they hope I can see something good that they don't see? I don't know.

If we're not proud of our work, it means we haven't really put ourselves into it and we certainly haven't followed our nature. Then it just becomes a mediocre delivery, same as all the others: half-assed, lifeless.

That goes for everyone, including me: Whenever I don't feel proud, I know I've done mediocre stuff. And it's not that it's an obligation to develop only exceptional things—sometimes it's okay to produce average outputs, if they're not that crucial—but you have to be aware of that.

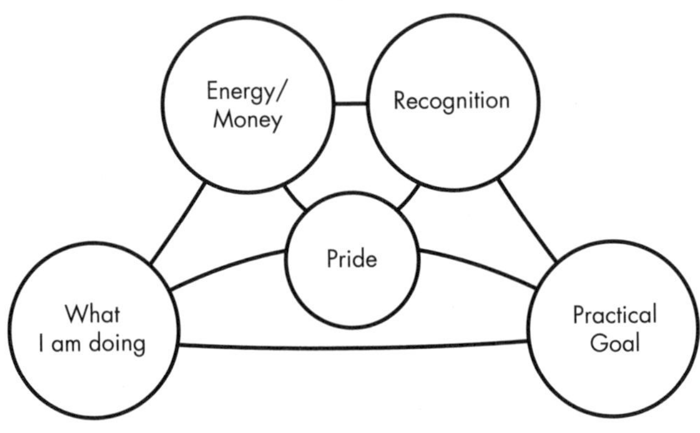

When I am well aligned, and it usually happens to me while I write the newsletter, or a book, but it also happens with less prestigious texts (like a sales email, for example), I reread and feel proud, very proud. This does not mean that what I wrote is perfect, on the contrary; it means that I am in it, that I feel the text is alive because I was alive when I was working on it. And it changes everything because I feel ready to defend my work, to enter the world with my head held high.

When we are proud of what we have done, we cherish it as a part of us. If someone tells me that Fabula's ads aren't great, I don't take it personally, I say, "Look, it works, and

I'm okay with that"; but if someone tells me the newsletter is crap, I'm ready to start a crusade. The same thing happened to me when an editor wrote me terrible things about Edito, our tool for editing: I was so proud of all the work done on the product, the care and attention poured into it, that I was ready to gouge his eyes out. It's not a matter of ego, mind you: It's a matter of steady feet, of not getting swerved by the winds of the world.

If what we have done is mediocre, we know it, we don't hold on, and we will be sucked into the storm.

But if we put ourselves in it, we take pride in it and claim our space, even if the space is as big as a tile, no one will be able to kick us out.

Ambush no. 12

Are you proud of who you are, what you have done, and what you are currently doing? Would you be willing to defend your work because you are sure of its authenticity? Would you invest your savings, or six months of your life, in the idea you have conceived? Do you have faith in what you have done?

If the answer is no, you risk entering the world looking arrogant and boastful, having nothing on your hands or having something you don't like, something that doesn't represent you, something that is just a waste of time.

Then you will feel fatigued, the money will not come, no one will be able to reassure you because you will not recognize yourself, and you will feel like a fraud. In short, it would be better to take two steps back. Ha ha.

Responsibility and cocreation of reality

During a shamanic training led by shaman and healer Foster Perry, I did a vision quest and spent twenty-four hours alone in the woods inside a circle I made out of branches. From dawn to dawn. Without food, phone, cigarettes. Just me, two bottles of water, a roll of toilet paper, a sleeping bag, and my drum. The goal: to stay awake the whole time, waiting, precisely, for a vision. The night was pitch black and, when I heard animal noises, I would beat the drum with all the strength I had to scare them away, shouting, "Get out of my circle! Stay out of my circle!"

In the morning, when I was walking back to the fire where I was going to meet with the other trainees, the shaman said, "Now you can be a man. You can cocreate reality." There and then I did not understand what he was trying to tell me. I just wanted to go have breakfast and get warm.

A few months later, I was in front of my house, it was 2 a.m., and I was chatting with a friend of mine. He was complaining about his business associates, about the insurmountable problems they were having with task management, their communication difficulties. I told him that if he had unresolved issues with them, it was better to talk about them openly, before the situation became unbearable; I explained to him that I did the exact thing with my partner at the time . . .

My friend nodded and replied, "You're lucky to have a partner like him . . ."

And that's when it happened.

The shaman's words came back from who knows where along with the sound of the drum I played like a madman all night long.

"This is nonsense," I told him, "I'm not just lucky. I decide what goes into my circle and what has to stay out. I am the one who creates my reality."

We can all do that: stand in the center of our circle and define what the reality around us will be like. We are the ones who choose to put up with that job, that relationship, that partner, that unmanageable situation. And we always have the power to push it away, to say, "No, I don't want to."

In the same way we can choose what to let into our lives: whether or not to write every morning, whether or not to be authentic, the kind of house we live in, the city, the people we love, the truth of seeing ourselves for who we are, the courage to express ourselves for real.

It is a constant responsibility and it is what determines our expansion and our impact in the world.

The drop I mentioned earlier, which falls and ripples the water, is us within our circle.

Now we just have to choose.

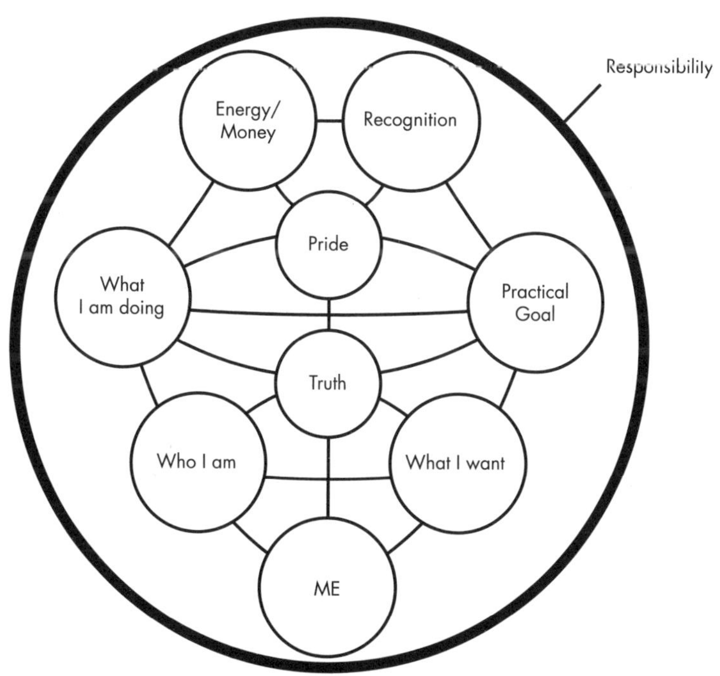

Ideals and impact

Our expansion does not only affect us: It has consequences within the world. It can generate well-being, disarray, happiness, sadness, and destruction, depending on our yearning, on why we decided to expand.

It is important that we ask ourselves:

- What impact do I want to make on the world?
- What do I believe in? (What are my ideals?)

If we are writers and we believe that literature is crucial in the development of humanity and our impact is to write a piece that moves people's spirits, we won't write a soft fantasy novel, and we certainly won't churn out one a year as best-selling writers do.

Instead, if we believe that the important thing is to have fun doing what we enjoy, and we want to bring that same entertainment to the millions of readers who are waiting for another one of our stories, that's when we will write a book a year!

If we are entrepreneurs and we believe that having a business means creating a workplace that both us and our employees can enjoy, the impact we will want to generate is to always pay salaries and do it on time, to provide security for families.

If, on the other hand, we believe that the important thing is the creative drive, if in our ideal workplace we work late in an attempt to truly express ourselves, the impact we would like to generate has nothing to do with material well-being and security but with ambition and overcoming limits.

We should not underestimate the importance of our ideals because it will always affect the kind of expansion we will have in the world.

For example, I know very well that I could create a Sefirot

line of educational games. I can put ten or twenty games a year into the market, and thus generate a very profitable new line of revenue. If my ideals were related to the concept of having a thriving business and paying salaries to as many people as possible, I wouldn't have too much trouble creating a product line like that. Instead, my ideals are less practical—it seems fair to me that one should aim to develop tools that can last over time—so it makes me sick to even think about making short-lived products just to build up numbers and revenue.

One is no better than the other (nor more noble). Both ideals harbor dangers: Those who want to generate wealth might not devote themselves to something they love for fear that it won't produce enough revenue; those who want to develop a great product that will last might then risk not selling enough.

I know full well that I could move the company abroad, pay fewer taxes, and streamline the paperwork that in Italy unfortunately takes a ridiculously long time. If my ideals were to maximize my income and that of my company, I would go abroad immediately. Instead, in my ideals there is a very strong sense of freedom, so the obligation of having to live abroad bothers me too much.

Recognizing our ideals and the impact we want to generate helps us through our path. We need to ask ourselves whether we are aligned with our ideals and, if not, find a way to rebalance and go along with them.

If I need to increase the company's sales but my ideals do not allow me to put random products into the market, I will try to develop something different, that can sell but that I also believe in.

If I want to be successful with my books but my ideals speak of high literature, I will try to write the best detective story that has ever seen the shelves of a bookstore, in an attempt to turn it into a cult.

- Who are we deep down?
- For what purpose have we come to this world?
- What do we want to experience?

These are the questions we must ask ourselves.
In the answer we will find our expansion.

Conclusions

The diagram represents a system that is constantly changing and readjusting. Whenever we feel lost, dissatisfied, or annoyed, we can try to understand which point is out of balance:

- Are we following our ideals?
- Are we telling the truth to ourselves?
- Are we proud of what we are doing?
- Are the expansion and impact we have in the world what we desired? And do we feel satisfied with them?

We must remember that it is always our responsibility; we are the ones who must choose to be aware of who we are and what we are doing.

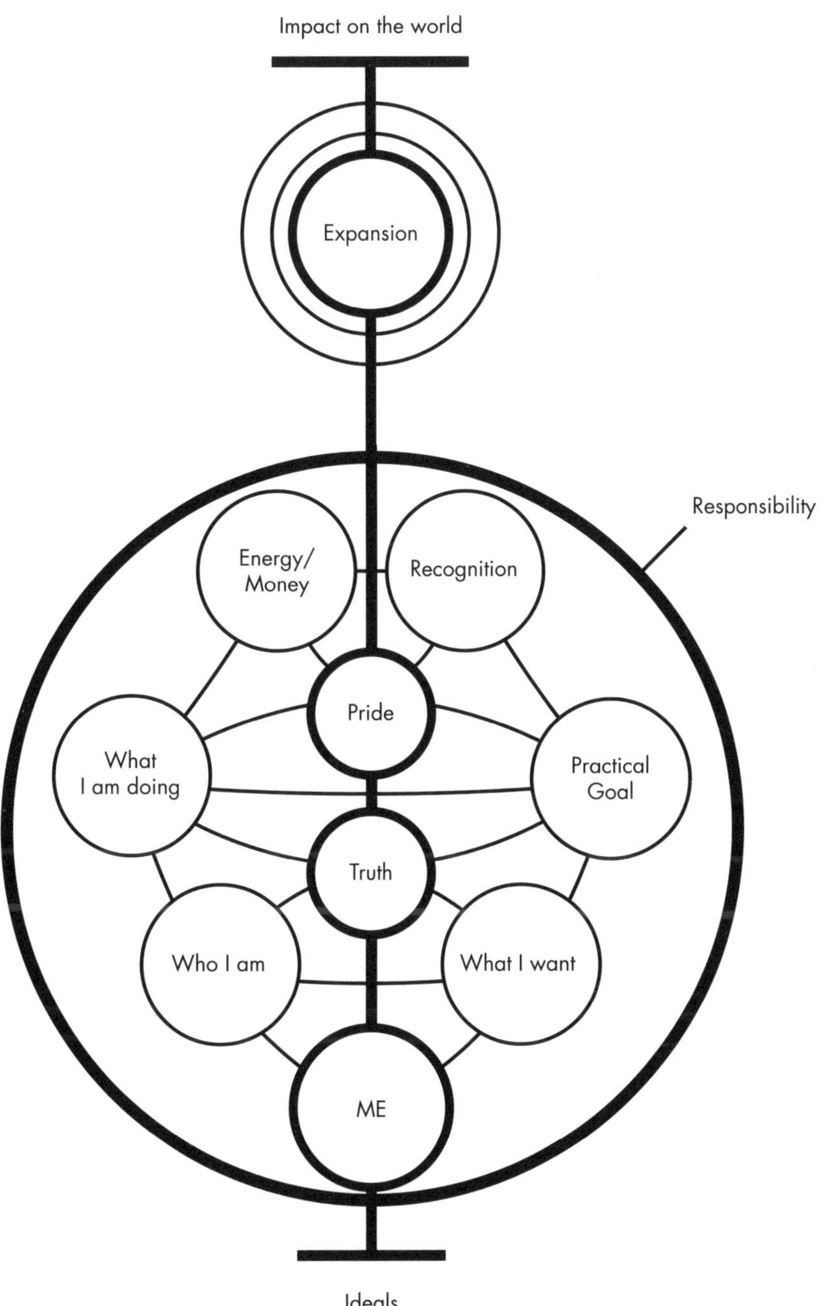
Impact on the world
Expansion
Responsibility
Energy/
Money
Recognition
Pride
What
I am doing
Practical
Goal
Truth
Who I am
What I want
ME
Ideals

The last ambush

When I moved to China to work for OnePlus (the cell phone company), I experienced two of the most peaceful months of my life. There wasn't much to do, so I spent half of every day sitting around or talking with my colleagues. My paycheck was always on time and it was a fat one, so I could afford to spend as much as I felt like without having to check my bank account. One day I realized that the box of fennel tea I had brought with me in case of nighttime stomach aches was still closed. At that moment, I realized that I had never felt anxious while in China: I had money, I was never asked for who knows what effort, I slept well.

But it wasn't the kind of life for me: Despite the peace of mind, I felt a gaping hole to fill, and I couldn't pretend it wasn't there as I sat warming my office chair. So I left.

I wanted to be creative; I wanted to live in uncertainty—ease wasn't my cup of tea.

The price of creativity is the constant ambush that you do to yourself. This book should teach you to ambush yourself, to be real, authentic, to shake yourself up and wake up, again and again, to go deep, when you stick to a secure job that doesn't let you express yourself, when you get lost behind useless excuses, when you dissipate chasing only material ambitions, when you don't express yourself to your full potential.

Some people may want to live in constant comfort, but the creative person does not like that. The creative likes adventure, the danger around the corner, the unbeaten road, the beast hiding in the dark, until they realize that they are, in fact, the beast lurking in the dark: never satiated, always moving and evolving.

It's no cakewalk, is it? That is precisely why you must take pride in it, know the price you pay, and value what you do—your freedom, your independence, your own way of writing, painting, inventing, living, creating. I'm not lying: It is something so true and precious and unparalleled that it must be preserved. You must cherish and respect it. It is you at your highest expansion, your highest potential, the power of your mind, heart, and hands, and the ability to generate something that can impact you and others.

You must take creativity very seriously. It is a game of life and such an important one. The game of children contributing to the universe. It was not there before, and now—poof—it is there.

Welcome, creatives.

PART VII

Random Lessons in Creativity

We're almost through with the book. I am a little sad since I feel that I still have a few things to say. So here you can find some thoughts, insights, further provocations, and practical, work-related advice that I think will be helpful.

Benchmarking, novelty, and theft

I often get mad at students and juniors for not doing what is called *benchmarking*, which is the study and comparison of competitors and similar products. Basically: If we are designing a plastic chair, we must study other plastic chairs; if we are designing a book, we must study other books. When I ask them why they had not done benchmarks, they would tell me that they wanted to develop something of their own, without outside influences, they wanted to be original and creative. That's when I reply, "Now take something you like and copy it, make it identical, steal it."

I often forced students to redo a logo by stealing someone else's style, even using the same colors and shapes. Or to redesign an app by tracing the colors and icons of Netflix or Spotify.

When people ask me why, I say, "How do you think we all learned?"

The first time I formatted one of my novels, I copied Feltrinelli's grid. I took a book I had at home that I liked (I think it was *Lands of Glass* by Baricco) and reproduced it on the layout software. But don't think it was a piece of cake! I spent hours and hours measuring the distances to the millimeter, trying to guess the font used and the line spacing. I did test after test and I . . . learned. Then I studied an Einaudi book, then an Adelphi book, so my eye became accustomed to the differences, to better understand some of the design choices, even the way I could place the numbers. Gradually, I was able to make autonomous choices that I liked.

Every product and piece around us—from the chair to the television, to the remote control, to the book, to the cell phone interface, to the illustration we see on Instagram—are created by skilled professionals, by people who are often more knowledgeable than we are or more talented, from whom we can learn and draw inspiration.

The great artists of the past went to ateliers and, for years, copied the works of the masters before, developing a style of their own, so we should not be afraid of either stealing or losing our originality. In fact, the exact opposite is true: We should absorb as much as possible, store, treasure, and humbly take as much as we can.

It is also important to draw our own personal line between theft and inspiration. Is it so terrible if someone discovered Fabula and decided to develop a similar tool for mail marketing? Would it be blatant copying or simple inspiration? Think of Goethe: If he had been stopped by the fear of being a "thief," we would not have his *Faust*, only Marlowe's. And the same goes for Thomas Mann, who came after them. And what about Satispay, a payments app that has taken over a single function of China's WeChat? What are they? Criminals or talented people who replicated a working system and managed to repurpose it in Italy?

What if we had a chance to freely rewrite *Harry Potter, The Hunger Games, The Catcher in the Rye, The Great Gatsby*? It wouldn't be creative work, some might say. So you say

Nolan's *Batmans* are not creative? Ha ha. Do you understand what nonsense and prejudice that is?

Copy, steal, take whatever you want, rework it, and don't be afraid. Get truly inspired.

Managing a creative team

I think this is one of the biggest challenges. I managed an in-house creative team at Sefirot for almost a year and then dismantled it because I had made too many mistakes. I mean, I spent over fifty thousand dollars to find out how unprepared I was to manage a creative team. Ha ha. It is a very difficult commitment because creativity cannot be enforced by coercion and control. Sure, one can force their employees or subordinates to have a fixed schedule and strict rules, but as effective as that may be in a classic office environment, it is not so great when it comes to creativity.

The problem is that creativity pokes its head out when people aim beyond mediocrity, beyond doing things just for the sake of it: It happens when they try to be proud; they want to take their phones and tell their friends, "Look at this cool thing I'm doing at work!"

But how do we get them to want to get there?

How can we convince the team we are leading (or paying) that if they really dive in, they will get more satisfaction?

I am convinced that, even within a team, creativity should

be inspired. People should want to excel, not so much for the company but for themselves, to grow and evolve, to improve and feel nurtured by what they are doing.

I often notice that pitches are sloppy, lazy, the ideas are banal, just a pile of junk written on a piece of paper—things that might be fine for a distracted boss, but that not even the creative people who proposed them would use for their own projects.

In those cases, I invite people to think, "Would you use these designs for your own company?" Usually, the person on the other side hesitates. "Then why should I use them for mine?" I add.

That's why I always suggest to all my students to launch and run their own project: to feel the level of attention rising and the desire to care about it, to make nurturing, well-thought-out choices, and then to learn how to bring that same attention to their everyday job.

One day a guy who was working as a project manager within a company told me that his own boss (the owner) was demanding too much of the team he was managing. I told him, "Let's play a game. Imagine that you own the company and your boss is a client who is getting annoyed with waiting for the delivery. How do you see the situation now?" He thought about it for a moment then widened his eyes and said, "This team is not working well at all!" Here we go.

Having worked both for a company and in an agency (usually in the company the work is done for a product that is sold, while in the agency the work is done for clients who request it) I realize that managing a team in the agency is easier because deadlines are imposed from the outside. In the company, on the other hand, everyone knows that if they were to be late, nothing would happen. And it's true: A product launch, unless publicly announced, can always be postponed.

Laughing with friends, I have often said that I should try to invent fictitious customers to use as motivation for my employees. In truth, I have not yet found an effective solution. For now I prefer to work with freelancers who, if nothing else, have an interest in delivering as soon as possible. It is not ideal but better than trying to convince your employees to be creative.

The other risk I ran in trying to inspire as much creativity and independence as possible was that the best employees at one point said to me, "Thanks for everything, I'm leaving and opening my own thing." I had inspired them too much. Ha ha.

Learn how to work

This is the most popular question among students. They bring me a hypothesis of a project, of an advertising campaign, of an app by showing me just one variant (which is usually no good), so I start firing off speculations out loud, as if I were improvising a brainstorming session, or I open their file and stand there changing the logo, generating new versions, comparing them.

They roll their eyes and ask me how to do what I'm doing: to pull out ideas so quickly, to create other versions, to dive in. They think it's some strange superpower that came out of who knows where.

I remember I had the same problem the first few years of college. I would get on Adobe Illustrator and design a logo and then stare at it again and again wondering how to make it better and thinking it sucked. Eventually, I would turn it in anyway, hoping my professor wouldn't notice that it was crap. Spoiler alert, the professor would notice.

What does it mean to learn how to work creatively?

It means learning to play with creative material: to say bullshit out loud, ideas for random ads, obscene and impractical concepts, crazy stuff, and to keep going and going at it, laughing, forgetting that we're sifting through the sieve looking for something and deliberately getting lost in a river. That's the change of outlook. To stop looking for the perfect logo as if it were an equation to be solved and instead to play with pen and paper with lines and shapes, and to have the will to do it for hours, nonstop, with passion.

That's why I always tell students, "Make a mess, get your hands dirty, play, have fun. Find fifty, a hundred proposals, and then choose five. And you will see that those five are special, and you won't need me to tell you—you will see it yourself."

Don't stop for any reason

When I was twenty-two years old, I decided that I would promote my novel through guerrilla marketing: I would allow people to download it for free from the site in e-book form, while I walked around Milan, dressed as a harlequin like the protagonist of my book, giving away flyers. The initial idea was also to print ten thousand leaflets and walk incessantly through the city and pin them up wherever I found space.

However, one day I had a doubt: Was it legal to put up posters around the city? I checked on the Internet and the answer was: No! Absolutely not! I would have had to put a sixteen dollar or so revenue stamp on each sheet, and if I didn't, I would have risked a fine of up to three hundred dollars for each poster I put up. I thought, "Well, just don't get caught," but no! They would have fined the beneficiary of the posting, namely me . . .

In the end, I desisted. I imagined I had to start my adult life with a debt of thirty million (three hundred dollars for ten thousand posters) and I chickened out. I simply gave out flyers and did not go ahead with hanging posters. And, of course, the handouts did not bring great results; in short, my guerrilla marketing was a flop.

That's one of my regrets. In retrospect, I say to myself, "Maybe it would have been better if I hadn't inquired." Or I could have found a ploy, made the site anonymous, with a pseudonym for the book and called it a day.

The point is that I let rules limit me.

This will always happen. If you raise your hand to say, "I have a new idea. Can I do it?" there will be someone who will promptly reply, "No!" and just kill you.

In 2013, I launched my first Kickstarter campaign for intùiti. At that time, you could not do it from Italy—you had to have a UK account—so being a completely oblivious twenty-four-year-old, I asked a friend who lived in London if he would lend me his account. Let's say it again: *if he would lend me his account*. Anyone who has gone to an accountant at least once has already understood the naivety and stupidity of my request. A month later, I had over forty thousand dollars land in his bank account. Fortunately, no one noticed (and enough years have passed that I feel comfortable talking about it); however, I am sure that if I had called my accountant, he would have told me, "No, Matteo, you can't do that. You'll get into trouble." And I wouldn't have launched the campaign.

The same happened with the opening of Sefirot. An e-commerce that sells worldwide from Italy was unheard of, impossible to comply with regulations, and so on. Eventually, I opened it and started selling and shipping. I thought, we'll find a way to adapt it later. And indeed we did find it.

There is a saying in America that goes: "Don't ask for permission, ask for forgiveness." And I think, with the proper adjustments, it makes a lot of sense. It takes very little to stop creativity, especially when it comes to bureaucratic nonsense.

Don't let anything stop you. There will always be someone ready to tell you that it can't be done, that it's risky, that it's a problem, that there is nothing that fits your specific situation or idea.

A friend of mine worked for months on a game with a similar dynamic to Jungle Speed. She did it out of passion, because she was having fun, and then she never pitched it to anyone because she was afraid someone would tell her, "This is plagiarism. You can't do it." That one thought brought everything down. And now that I see dozens of games that trace the same idea as Cards Against Humanity or other famous games, I think, "Clearly it could have been done."

Personally, every time I have a similar doubt, I ask myself, "What would be worse: to do it and be slapped on the wrist, or not to do it?"

Not doing it. That way, we lose from the start.

Find your voice (a.k.a., everything but the oink)

There is a lot of talk in literature about writers' quests to find their voice—that unique way of writing and tone that defines the style and makes it recognizable and valuable. The same can be said of any creative field, of the "voice" (or style) of painters, sculptors, illustrators, and designers.

I believe that voice is a collection of our authentic qualities, our way of acting, of being. A writer who likes complex plots and plot twists and is not very fond of descriptions will find their voice when they begin to focus on what they do best. A writer who values the inner workings and the psychology of characters will also find their voice by delving into those depths.

Who are we? What do we love? We have to go in that direction, and we have to do it in all areas.

I also believe that our voice has to align with what we can do and with our limitations. We have to be able to find our talents and use them to the best of our ability. When I say, "Everything but the oink," I mean that we are the pigs.

Let me give you an example: I am not an illustrator. I don't know how to do it. If someone were to commission a work from me, I wouldn't really know how to manage. Yet I have illustrated intùiti, and I have done the same thing with the UX manual and with the vignettes in this book. I can do that: thick lines, solid colors, simple drawings. I am not able to go in a different direction (and I'm also not interested). If I accept that, I can optimize that style of illustration and use it for what I need. I can find my own recognizable voice.

The same goes for the way I design logos and graphics. If you compare Fabula, intùiti, Cicero, Edito, you can see that the hand is the same, a hand that wants to go in the direction of simplicity and minimalism, both because I like it that way but also because I would struggle to move in any other direction!

For the covers of the *Mario* series it is the same. I don't know how to paint, and I don't have any technique; however, I can paint using a few colors and drawing big, ill-defined shapes. That's fine: I can go in that direction and get an acceptable result.

Don't let your limitations stop you: Welcome them and cherish them. Use them to express yourself. Are you only capable of making trivial illustrations with a few geometric lines? Develop that style! The only illustrations you know how to do are vector illustrations? Perfect, go that way! Are you good at ink drawing, collage, or pencil? Okay! You can't do it yourself but you are good at giving prompts to Dall-e or other AI systems? That's okay too.

In short, find out who you are and get to the bottom of it, and use everything you have and like without any shame.

Creating something new and other people's anger

The first version of the *Survival Guide for UX Designers,* a book where I simplified the concept of UX design and I brought it back to a dimension of good design, was released for free online and it got thousands of downloads and received a good amount of hate inside UX designer groups. It was mostly professors from universities and members of UX associations who were the most outraged: They wrote that I was incompetent, stupid, someone seeking easy fame, and other less elaborate insults.

The same thing happened when we published Fabula, receiving indignation and anger from writers and writing professors telling us that it made no sense to follow a structure to write a story.

And once again when we released Edito, editors from well-known publishing houses criticized every aspect of the product (without even having used it), and they did it with a lot of vigor.

If you create something new, rest assured that someone will be upset. Ha ha. And I'll tell you more: An emotional reaction is the best appreciation people can give you since it is a symptom that you have done a great job. It means you have hit the right spot: the issue that was distressing them unconsciously, a raw nerve they wanted to hide at all costs, or something they are frightened by in what you are saying or presenting.

Are you taking business away from them? Their authority? Credibility? Market? Opportunities? Certainty?

If they think you're depriving them of something, it means you've hit the jackpot; the product works. In fact, the UX manual has become the best-selling manual in Italy; Fabula was a great success; Edito gets compliments from all the professionals who use it.

I'm telling you this to help you withstand the other side of success: Receiving anger and outrage is a heavy burden to carry. When I read the comments from UX experts saying I was a jerk, I was hurt. I tried to laugh it off, not to look, not to respond; however, the pain hits all the same. I had written a free manual, I had poured my heart into it, and they were stomping on it. When I saw the public attack on Facebook by a major editor against Edito, my skin was thicker. I wrote to him, "You're talking without having used the product. I'll send you a deck," and later he replied, "It's a good product. Sorry, if you want I'll remove the post." But by then the damage was done, the energy had been wasted, and he could not return it to me.

It's not easy to be creative, because we are constantly exposing ourselves to the outside world, exposing a part of us that will be at the mercy of everyone who feels like taking a peek and saying it's crap.

Yet that's part of the game. Don't let the first person who comes by stop you; no matter who they are, stick to what you've done. Do you like it? Are you proud of it? Does it represent you?

To hell with everybody else.

The channel is the creativity

Before opening Sefirot, I often found writing and developing independent products very frustrating. I would make an effort to write a novel, send it to publishers whose websites stated, "We will give you a feedback in six to nine months," and I would become discouraged. What was I supposed to do while I waited? Write another novel? I didn't feel like it. The same was happening with Kickstarter campaigns. I raised almost fifty thousand dollars for intùiti . . . and then what? No publishing house contacted me to say, "That's cool, we'll publish it. Make another tool!" If I wanted to create a new product, I would have had to do the work all over again. It was such a struggle. So I would go through periods of creative flair, where I would develop, make, build, launch, and then I had entire months of despair, where I would ask myself, "What's the point of all this? What am I using my creativity for?" It felt like I could not build a channel into which I could fit what I was doing, and it required more and more energy to start the process over again each time.

Of course, I used to tell myself, "You are doing it for yourself"; however, it did not give me enough consolation during the dark times. All I could see was darkness.

After Sefirot opened, I experienced a new feeling: that of having a channel ready to welcome me. I would still have to struggle with the production and implementation of a new product, but I knew it would have its own outreach into the world. And that took the stress off the creative drive—it made it more fluid and immediate. It took away a major worry from my whole process: beating around the bush unnecessarily.

Having a functioning channel instigates creativity. Think of writers like Fitzgerald who wrote short stories like it was a job because he got paid by magazines for them, or employees of game companies who are called upon to develop dozens of concepts a year. Not all of them will be brilliant; however, in the midst and in the chaos, some pearls have come out: This great movement fosters the flow of creativity.

When the editor at Hoepli called me to say, "Matteo, we want you to write the new edition of our UX manual," I said yes but I was not too convinced. If he had not proposed it to me, I would not have thought about it. However, knowing that I had a channel, I set to work, and I must say that I was amazed by the result. I realized that there was a missing piece in the first edition, and I was happy to fill the hole.

Create a channel, even a small and private one, print thirty copies of your novel and give it to friends, find a publishing house to work with, a literary agent, get used to launching projects on Kickstarter. In short, make sure that you have an extra stimulus to tickle your creativity instead of tearing it down.

The money issue

When I was twenty-two, I worked at the Fuorisalone in Milan—five days of standing around checking tickets to earn three hundred dollars. As soon as the gig ended, I walked into a print shop in Bovisa, near the university, and negotiated those three hundred dollars in exchange for one hundred photocopies of my latest manuscript. Then, I took those copies and left them on the benches in Parco Sempione. Ten years later, I met a girl who had found one of those manuscripts—and still remembered it.

To print intùiti, after the first Kickstarter production was sold out, I had to make a new small production, spending four thousand dollars (and at the time my salary was 1,600 a month).

To distribute Sefirot products, from 2018 to 2024 we spent over two million dollars; this money allowed one hundred fifty thousand people to get connected with tools that helped them create, write, launch their projects, etc. Not only that: We reinvested the earnings to develop new products and courses, and to pay professionals of all sorts.

Often in the creative field, the role of money is misunderstood: It is seen as vile, dirty, rarely to be mentioned and to be accumulated secretly and with shame. In the publishing world, for example, Lord forbid anyone talk of a book as a product that sells! And it seems to be a matter of pride to work for glory and not for adequate compensation for one's efforts and skills.

Money is energy. Money is given to us in exchange for our energy, and it is, in turn, energy that we reuse to eat, sleep, entertain ourselves, or create new energy.

The three hundred dollars earned at the Fuorisalone was my energy from five days spent on my feet, and without that, I would not have been able to print my manuscript. The same goes for the four thousand dollars—two and a half months of my work at that time—without which intùiti would have been dead. And I will spare you the calculation for the two million.

When I invested that money, friends and relatives looked at me like I had lost it. And, if I had also looked at money only as money, I would never have done that. Come on, how can you really think of emptying your pockets for one hundred copies of your manuscript to give away at a park?

Instead, if we start to see money for what it is—energy to do things—we can open our wallets and buy those canvases we like, those colors we need, print copies of our book even if we don't know who to give them to, or pay for an English translation. In short, we can make energy circulate.

I often ask my students, "Would you invest your savings on this project?"

It's just a way of pushing them around, the real question is: "Would you invest your vital energy, your time, on this?"

Your energy permeates what you create. How much is a deck of intùiti worth? If we think of it as just seventy-eight cards printed and packed inside another piece of printed, folded, and glued cardboard, its value is nothing. A few dollars worth of paper. But inside you can find two years worth of my energy. The same goes for our other products, and for your products! For your works. For your books. For your efforts.

Money is no longer a vile commodity. It is a recognition, a return of energy, and a chance to be able to continue doing what you do. A writer who earns money from their books can devote themselves to being a writer, instead of having to teach to eat and pay the bills.

We have to accept the money, wait for it with open arms as something good and vital, and with the same open arms, we have to be willing to put it back into circulation.

"What if someone steals my idea?"

There is always someone in class or during lectures who hesitantly raises their hand to ask, "What if someone steals my idea?"

They are afraid to send a manuscript to a publishing house, or to talk about their project with others, they would get as far as having friends sign NDAs.

The problem with ideas is that if we don't have any we don't go anywhere; however, with the idea alone we don't do anything with it. Ideas alone are worth nothing.

Think of how much energy, commitment, and faith is required to bring an idea to fruition . . . but who would go through the trouble of stealing something unfinished from us and then investing resources to bring it to life? If someone stole the idea of a product from us and then committed months, years, to develop it and then to distribute it, we would almost have to go and shake their hand for their perseverance.

Execution matters much more than the idea. If we develop a branding tool and someone else comes along and does the same thing but better, communicating it better, with more funding, stronger partnerships, etc., they win. Did they copy the idea? Maybe. Did they execute it better? Apparently so.

Anyone can go listen to startup pitches and steal their ideas. Anyone can see a product or service in the big world of the Internet and decide to develop something similar. Anyone can have an idea similar to yours for a book or a painting or who knows what else.

Do not be afraid. You will take inspiration from others, and they will take inspiration from you. They will copy you. They will steal your ideas. They will try to imitate you or do better. And you will be angry, you will be furious, you will be hurt.

When another online UX academy entered the market, I was furious because they stole the texts of my advertisements (they were identical) that had cost me months of testing and effort. I wanted to strangle them because the pages also had a similar way of communicating. But I stopped myself thinking that I had done the same, taking inspiration from American academies.

Over time, I discovered that it is nice to have competitors, a company that comes out of nowhere, grows by stealing or taking inspiration from us, and then one day becomes better than us, and finds a way to outperform us. It's nice because it becomes an exchange: At that point it's us who can steal from them, copy from them, and do better than them. Ha ha.

Where do creative blocks come from?

After reading passages in this book some of my friends asked me, “Where do the blocks come from? Why do they occur?”

It is impossible to give a one-size-fits-all answer. There is something, at some point, that gets stuck so the wheel doesn’t turn, and we start looking at the symptom we perceive, thinking that’s the problem—but in truth, the block is somewhere else, light years away. We think the problem is the book we can’t write, but really the issue is the lack of confidence we have in the publishing world. We think the problem is our partner with whom we argue every day, but in truth, it is that we are afraid to be alone. We think it is A when in fact it is B.

When people tell me that intùiti nights feel a bit like psychoanalysis sessions, it’s true: It’s about going deep, looking for the roots of the reasons why we feel like rusty pivots. It is painful because it means going to rummage through uncomfortable, sharp, sometimes explosive truths. Blocks due to family, dads, moms, children, partners, or our own insecurities, or laziness. Yet when the blockage is brought to light, I guarantee it is not that awful, it is like when you get a tooth pulled; suddenly you are relieved.

I have been struggling with Sefirot for three years now, something is wrong but not with the company, it is within me (it is never others, it is always us). After the first two years of abundance, Facebook and Instagram changed as a result of the advent of iOS 14 and our margins decreased considerably.

The company's growth was halted by external causes. And I spent three years, particularly the last year and a half, worrying about building a team that could deal with this invisible enemy: the Facebook algorithm. I became obsessed with it, trying to find new sources of revenue, new channels, new ways to sell and sell and sell. And now I wonder what's creative about what I do. I have developed two products in the last three years. Too little, for a company that makes creative tools. Where is the research? Where is the power of creativity?

Where have I lost it?

That is the profound question. Where did I gamble much of my creativity to become a marketer? If I stop and think about what I would do if Sefirot billed three million a year, and then even more—six million, ten million—would I stop being frustrated and stop chasing growth? And the answer is no: The itch of dissatisfaction I feel would continue indefinitely.

I am the one who is not shining as brightly as I could. And I feel it.

To understand, one must go through what happened step by step. What did I desire when I opened the company? I craved social revenge, I remember that. But what did I want? To fill the market with my products and have fun. To have a channel, a relationship with the world. And then what got me? The eagerness, of course. I felt so cool that I didn't want to get off the podium that I had built for myself. I wanted to become a leader in the creative world. I wanted to sell millions of products. I created a beast made of fire that I needed to feed only to realize that it could never be satiated. I had to make products to spin the wheel, to feed the fire, and . . . the desire began to fade. It seemed to me that my products lost their soul, they became pieces of coal made for the train of capitalism.

What did I want when I opened Sefirot?

To express myself. That was all I wanted.

And I didn't realize that I had built the channel I so desperately wanted. Those things I desperately needed when I was twenty-three years old and trying to distribute intùiti—the money for production and the people to reach—are now here, ready for me. And I didn't see it for three years. I kept living like I had to push and push and push, when I could finally really expand, lock myself in, hatch like a creative, and then come back with new products, new books, new ideas.

I realized this last night. Five years ago, Matteo would have said, "Oh, my god, my god, I can finally do anything I want!"

It was liberating. I stopped and said to myself, "Now you can really be creative. You have the channel, you have the resources. No one can stop you." There it was. Somebody always prevented me, and I believed it. So I always prevented myself.

Go back, search where you dare not to look, admit what you dare not to admit. Put yourselves under the magnifying glass. Why have you lost your drive? What were you told as children? What did you learn to repeat to yourselves again and again like a mantra? How come you neutered yourselves?

Ideas that work and ideas that don't matter if they work

There are contexts in which the ideas we decide to pursue must work. Typically this term, *to work*, refers to the material realm, to a business vision, whereby products and services must generate value. Then the ideas must make sense for a specific target audience, address certain needs, have a market, a positioning, and a system in order to generate a return.

Very often, when we consider whether to take an idea forward and invest time on it (especially in business), it is almost necessary that the idea has to work, because otherwise we risk throwing away resources or getting yelled at by our supervisors or even losing a customer.

There is nothing wrong with pursuing only those ideas that work. Fabula, BAD, and Edito are examples of ideas that make sense and work; in fact, they were not risky investments. A manual on a trending topic, like artificial intelligence, or a bakery for celiacs, are also ideas that work.

However, we do not have to stop there. There are many ideas, often the best ones, which we may not care if they work or not. Writing an autobiographical book, for example, or a story that we would like to read. Or developing an idea that solves a personal need, without letting the thought that it might be ours alone stop us, even if it has no clear market. There are things through which we want to express ourselves regardless of the outcome. If I set out to paint a picture, or write a short story, or even work on a deck of cards for creativity out of my own personal need, free from any external expectation, from the ambition of the material world, it is not a bad thing, on the contrary.

I wrote two urban fantasy novels for this reason. I already knew it would be difficult to find a publisher since they did not accurately mirror the genre (and, in fact, my agent is still looking); however, I wrote them anyway because I wanted to live that story. I wanted to. I'm sure someone else will like it too, but primarily it was for me. I got emotionally attached to the characters; I got involved with them. Fuck the market.

The same thing happened with intùiti. A quick evaluation? Too secular to be a tarot deck. Too esoteric to be a corporate tool. Too complex for a broad target audience that doesn't feel like reading a two-hundred-odd-page manual. Too deep, it might scare off part of the target audience. An idea that would be wise not to work on.

Who cares? I wanted intùiti for myself. Sure, it would have helped other people but mostly I wanted it for me. I use intùiti every day, I would have bought it and studied it if another Matteo had made it.

The most creative ideas are the ones that solve our own needs. They come with high risks—economically and timewise, as we might invest resources for nothing, and emotionally, as we might feel desperate when no one else appreciates or understands us. But what a thrill! Ha ha.

Don't dismiss these ideas or wish them away, even if they scare us. Let's keep them there for a while, let's cuddle them, let's be tempted by creativity without safety nets and without meaning, the kind we can really fall into, the kind that pushes us toward projects we will hold on to like they are our own children.

Let's remember that thinking in business terms makes sense, but creativity . . . creativity doesn't give a damn about making sense.

PART VIII

Appendices

Finding teachers

My early readers were very fascinated by the figure of my teacher and asked me, “How do you find a teacher? Do I need to actively search for one, or will they come on their own?”

I believe that teachers appear when we are ready to listen. I met mine because I wanted to create intùiti. The first question she asked me was: “Do you know what tarot cards are?” I lifted my shirt to show her the inside of my arm, where I had a tattoo of the card depicting The Fool.

That was my story: I was desperately trying to express myself, and she arrived at the right moment. I’m sure others have completely different stories, but all I can say is this: Keep your eyes, heart, and ears wide open. And if your teacher appears, don’t let them slip away.

It is up to you to recognize them because they won’t try to be heard at all costs. If you don’t see them, teachers will move along and leave.

On inner work

In this text, I often refer to inner work because, over the years, I have been fortunate enough to engage in practices and techniques that have helped me release my blocks, become more authentic, and feel more deeply.

I encourage you to try them; I highly recommend it. I am convinced that creatives who work on themselves are more self-aware creatives.

For those who want to delve deeper, here is a list of what has worked for me, with the hope that it might also be helpful to you:

- Shamanic journeys with the drum
- Bioenergetics
- Tarot
- Sweat lodges
- Vipassana meditation
- Osho's dynamic meditations (especially kundalini)
- The chair technique (an exercise from Gestalt therapy)
- Family constellations

As for what I have written from page 120 to page 141, the content is drawn from the work of Alessandra Mazzucchelli, creative director, lecturer at the Polytechnic University of Milan, and author of many major advertising campaigns in the 1980s and 1990s. She continues to lead seminars on interpersonal communication to this day.

Useful books

There is no official bibliography for this text, but I thought I would compile a list of books that have inspired me and that I believe can open minds.

Castaneda, Carlos. *The Teachings of Don Juan: A Yaqui Way of Knowledge.* Washington Square Press, 1985.

Hillman, James. *The Soul's Code: In Search of Character and Calling.* Bantam, 1997.

Jodorowsky, Alejandro, and Marianne Costa. *The Way of Tarot: The Spiritual Teacher in the Cards.* Destiny Books, 2009.

Jodorowsky, Alejandro. *The Spiritual Journey of Alejandro Jodorowsky: The Creator of El Topo.* Park Street Press, 2008.

Lowen, Alexander. *Fear of Life.* The Alexander Lowen Foundation, 2012.

Munari, Bruno. *Design as Art.* Penguin Books, 2019.

Shinn, Florence Scovel. *The Game of Life and How to Play It.* DeVorss Publications, 1978.

Sibaldi, Igor. *I maestri invisibili. Come incontrare gli Spiriti guida.* Mondadori, 2021.

Sibaldi, Igor. *Libro degli angeli e dell'Io celeste.* Sperling & Kupfer, 2017.

Acknowledgments

To Alessandra Mazzucchelli, who taught me to set ambushes. Without her, I wouldn't be who I am today.

To Gaia, who was present throughout the first draft.

To Cristina and Umberto, who were the first to read it, be moved by it, and put it into practice. That's why I wrote it.

To Alizé, who translated it into English while preserving its energy and spirit.

To all my teachers, who have helped shape my journey.

To all the colleagues I've had over the years, and to the friends and acquaintances who had the courage to open up during the intùiti evenings.

To everyone who worked on this book: those who edited it, formatted it, and printed it.

Thank you.

May this book
help you become
your favorite creative.